MIRACULOUS HEALING FOR THE CHURCH

My People will be delivered and become a blessing in the Earth!

Miraculous Healing for the Church

incorporating
Your Personal Journal of Deliverance

JAMES GLOVER

PREMIER PUBLICATIONS
Helensburgh

Published by Premier Publications
P.O. Box 26623, Helensburgh G84 4AH

ISBN   0 9551605 0 2 (10 digit)
          978 0 9551605 0 9 (13 digit)

Printed in Great Britain.

Contents

Be Healed in the Name of Jesus Christ!

It is likely that you will consider reading this book for one of two reasons: either you are suffering from a sickness, disease, injury or disability, or you know someone else who is. There is no substitute for the Word of God on the subject of sickness and healing and all references, ideas, insights and wisdom defer both to the Bible and the revelation of the nature of our Heavenly Father.

This book is for those who are seeking to be healed by divine intervention and also for those who desire to be instruments of miraculous healing to others. We focus primarily on the Christian family because there are widespread problems with ill health among us.

Before you begin to read, it is strongly recommended that you go before the throne of God specifically to ask that He grant you both the ears to hear and the eyes to see. This will stir up the Spirit of God within you to bring to your attention those parts you need to discern for your eventual recovery.

Do not be deceived; this is no quick fix. You will find yourself challenged on many different issues. You may have to unlearn cherished beliefs, traditions and doctrines. To look at both your personal situation and the world around you through the eyes of Christ, to think as He does and to do things His way. God will definitely heal you; but He will do it the way He has always done it . . . from the inside.

In short, your mission (if you choose to accept it) is to put on the mind of Christ.

GOD IS SPEAKING
ARE we LISTENING

CHAPTER ONE

Why Do We Get Sick?

Ask a doctor that question and he will regale you with facts about biology, chemistry and physics. He will produce charts, X-rays, lab tests and scientific theory couched in latin names to try and explain your condition. His assessment may be accurate, his diagnosis clear and his recommended course of treatment, sound. But, according to our Creator, there is a simple one word explanation for physical, mental and psychological impairment: Sin! **Jn 5** "*5Now there was a certain man who had an infirmity thirty-eight years. 6When Jesus saw him lying there, and knew that he already had been in that condition a long time, He said to him, 'Do you want to be made well?' 8Jesus said to him, 'Rise, take up your bed and walk.' 9And immediately the man was made well, took up his bed, and walked. 14Afterward Jesus found him in the temple, and said to him, 'See, you have been made well. Sin no more, lest a worse thing come upon you'.*"

At this point, it would be useful for you to skim through the four gospels of Matthew, Mark, Luke and John and note what Jesus said nearly every time he healed someone. Simply put: Miraculous healing without forgiveness of sin is impossible. **Ps 103** "*2Bless the Lord, O my soul, And forget not all His benefits: 3Who forgives all your iniquities, Who heals all your diseases, 4Who redeems your life from destruction, Who crowns you with loving kindness and tender mercies.*"

In the scriptures we sometimes see apparent contradictions. One such incident can be found in **John 9** "*1Now as Jesus passed by, He saw* *a man who was blind from birth. ²And His disciples asked Him, saying, 'Rabbi, who sinned, this man or his parents, that he was born blind?' ³Jesus answered, 'Neither this man nor his parents sinned, but that the works of God should be revealed in him'."* How can Jesus say this when so many other scriptures teach otherwise? Did He make a mistake or is there a mistranslation?

This is wisdom: The Word of God is perfect, but we frequently mis-interpret what is being said. You cannot build a doctrine around one scripture, or dismiss promises on the basis of one or two seemingly contradictory scriptures.

Yet, many in the Church have done exactly that. Some have assumed that people get sick because that's the will of God, or they're born with a defect and that's their lot in life so they should just accept it and they use **John 9:1–3** to justify this position. Nothing could be fur-ther from the truth. The disciples wanted to know what sins could be attributed to this man's condition (Note: a very judgemental approach which is alive and well in many churches today). Jesus specifically answered their question, but in doing so he was not implying that this man and his parents were sinless.

He then goes onto say something which is deeply profound. Remember God is the Creator, nothing exists without Him including all the consequences that result from wrong living and wrong actions. He created those consequences so that He could also reveal His mercy and judgement at the appropriate time, which is why Jesus then goes on to say: *"⁴I must work the works of Him who sent Me while it is day; the night is coming when no one can work. ⁵As long as I am in the world, I am the light of the world."* **(Jn 9)**

At the time of writing, there are approximately six billion people alive on earth. Every single person, regardless of their stature in life is a sinner. **Ro 3** *"²³for all have sinned and fall short of the glory of God,"* Okay. So what about Christians? Are we, as Christians, sinless? **1 Jn 1** *"⁸If we say that we have no sin, we deceive ourselves, and the truth is not in us. ⁹If we confess our sins, He is faithful and just to forgive us our sins*

Personal Notes

You are seeking guidance from God to deal with your personal situation or that of a loved one. What has stood out for you so far? What questions have come to mind? Write these questions and comments down before you go any further.

These pages are your personal journal of deliverance, your future testimony, your record of God's grace. Don't skip over this part. Write down what the Holy Spirit is saying to you.

PRAYER – IF I REGARD INIQUITY IN MY HEART THE LORD WILL NOT HEAR ME

YAHWEH IS MY HEALER

PS. BEFORE I WAS AFLICTED I WENT ASTRAY

and to cleanse us from all unrighteousness. *¹⁰If we say that we have not sinned, we make Him a liar, and His word is not in us.*" Absolutely not, so the scripture says. We live under grace, or a perpetual state of forgiveness, but there is not a day that goes by when we do not have to confess our sins before God. We are certainly not perfect, but we aspire to perfection. **1 Jn 2** "*⁵But whoever keeps His word, truly the love of God is perfected in him. By this we know that we are in Him. ⁶He who says he abides in Him ought himself also to walk just as He walked.*"

So, what is sin? Some define it simply as the transgression of the laws of God. Well, that's a good starting point, but it is by no means the whole story. Human nature, even at its very best, is hostile toward God. **1 Jn 2** "*¹⁶For all that is in the world – the lust of the flesh, the lust of the eyes, and the pride of life – is not of the Father but is of the world.*" It's a spirit of rebellion, self reliance and self aggrandisement. It is the antithesis of loving God and your fellow man. Every thought, word and deed that elevates itself above the ways of God is sin and ultimately leads to death. **Mat 15** "*¹⁸But those things which proceed out of the mouth come from the heart, and they defile a man. ¹⁹For out of the heart proceed evil thoughts, murders, adulteries, fornications, thefts, false witness, blasphemies. ²⁰These are the things which defile a man,*" Put another way, we were all condemned from the moment we entered this world. **Ps 90** "*¹⁰The days of our lives are seventy years; And if by reason of strength they are eighty years, Yet their boast is only labour and sorrow; For it is soon cut off, and we fly away.*" **Jn 3** "*¹⁹And this is the condemnation, that the light has come into the world, and men loved darkness rather than light, because their deeds were evil.*"

Of course, as human beings, we might say, "Well, it's one thing to tell a lie but quite another to murder someone." And that would be right, at least on one level. There is a spiritual law that governs our behaviour. We can, without knowing it, do something right and receive a blessing for it now in this lifetime. Or, we can do something right intentionally, without the guidance of the Holy Spirit, and be blessed in this lifetime. This applies to all human beings. On the other hand we can do something wrong intentionally, or otherwise and receive the punishment for it now in this lifetime. **Ro 2** "*⁵But in*

Personal Notes

You are seeking guidance from God to deal with your personal situation or that of a loved one. What has stood out for you so far? What questions have come to mind? Write these questions and comments down before you go any further.

These pages are your personal journal of deliverance, your future testimony, your record of God's grace. Don't skip over this part. Write down what the Holy Spirit is saying to you.

accordance with your hardness and your impenitent heart you are treasuring up for yourself wrath in the day of wrath and revelation of the righteous judgement of God, ⁶*who 'will render to each one according to his deeds'."* **Gal 6** *"⁷Do not be deceived, God is not mocked; for whatever a man sows, that he will also reap."* Also, read the book of Deuteronomy for some excellent examples of how this works.

So, are we saying that everyone who becomes sick is guilty of some wicked personal sin? No, not necessarily. After all, how can a six-month-old child be held to that standard? But there is wrong-doing that results in what are called generational curses, which are carried through up to the third or fourth generation. **Ex 34** *"⁷keeping mercy for thousands, forgiving iniquity and transgression and sin, by no means clearing the guilty, visiting the iniquity of the fathers upon the children and the children's children to the third and the fourth generation."* Some children are born under a curse that had nothing to do with their free-will decisions. **Dt 5** *"⁹you shall not bow down to them nor serve them. For I, the Lord your God, am a jealous God, visiting the iniquity of the fathers upon the children to the third and fourth generations of those who hate Me,"* Their condition can be traced back to their parents, grandparents or great grandparents. No one escapes the consequences of the law through wrong-doing and all too often, it is their children and their children's children who end up paying the price for their actions. The consequences of sin frequently manifests itself as illness, injury that doesn't heal, disability, psychological disfunction, early death, poverty, violence and all manner of pain. (See **Deuteronomy 28:5–68** for a comprehensive list)

One more very important point on this subject. These consequences very rarely take place immediately, sometimes a whole generation can pass before the full force of the law is brought to bear on the sinner's descendants. **Jer 32** *"¹⁷Ah, Lord God! Behold, You have made the heavens and the earth by Your great power and outstretched arm. There is nothing too hard for You. ¹⁸You show loving kindness to thousands, and repay the iniquity of the fathers into the bosom of their children after them. The Great, the Mighty God, whose name is the Lord of hosts."* Make no mistake, every defect in the physiological and psychological make

Personal Notes

You are seeking guidance from God to deal with your personal situation or that of a loved one. What has stood out for you so far? What questions have come to mind? Write these questions and comments down before you go any further.

These pages are your personal journal of deliverance, your future testimony, your record of God's grace. Don't skip over this part. Write down what the Holy Spirit is saying to you.

up of every sick and distressed person on this planet is down to sin. There are degrees of consequence but guilt is universal.

Mental illness in all its forms, especially depression is another little-understood phenomenon. Touted medical "cures" may relieve some of the symptoms but do little to remove it completely. Demonic possession is not the myth that many would have you believe; it does exist. **1 Sa 16** *"14But the Spirit of the Lord departed from Saul, and a distressing spirit from the Lord troubled him. 15And Saul's servants said to him, 'Surely, a distressing spirit from God is troubling you'."* However it is not manifested in some of the ways that Hollywood would have you believe. Let's examine this subject a little more closely.

The Bible reveals that a being called Satan is the enemy of both God and man, that he once held a very high position in the angelic kingdom. Before God created man, the earth was populated by a third of all the angels and Lucifer (as he was called then) had rulership over them. Pride grew in Lucifer and he determined to take over the throne of God and turned all the angels on earth against God. He then led them in an attempt to overthrow God and claim the throne for himself, but he and his angels were cast back down to earth. The fact is they are still here today!

Rev 12 *"3And another sign appeared in heaven: behold, a great, fiery red dragon having seven heads and ten horns, and seven diadems on his heads. 4His tail drew a third of the stars of heaven and threw them to the earth. 7And war broke out in heaven: Michael and his angels fought with the dragon; and the dragon and his angels fought, 8but they did not prevail, nor was a place found for them in heaven any longer. 9So the great dragon was cast out, that serpent of old, called the Devil and Satan, who deceives the whole world; he was cast to the earth, and his angels were cast out with him."*

Lk 10 *"17Then the seventy returned with joy, saying, 'Lord, even the demons are subject to us in Your name.' 18And He said to them, 'I saw Satan fall like lightning from heaven'."*

Personal Notes

You are seeking guidance from God to deal with your personal situation or that of a loved one. What has stood out for you so far? What questions have come to mind? Write these questions and comments down before you go any further.

These pages are your personal journal of deliverance, your future testimony, your record of God's grace. Don't skip over this part. Write down what the Holy Spirit is saying to you.

Isa 14 *"¹²How you are fallen from heaven, O Lucifer, son of the morning! How you are cut down to the ground, You who weakened the nations! ¹³For you have said in your heart: 'I will ascend into heaven, I will exalt my throne above the stars of God; I will also sit on the mount of the congregation On the farthest sides of the north; ¹⁴I will ascend above the heights of the clouds, I will be like the Most High.' ¹⁵Yet you shall be brought down to Sheol, To the lowest depths of the Pit. ¹⁶Those who see you will gaze at you, And consider you, saying: 'Is this the man who made the earth tremble, Who shook kingdoms, ¹⁷Who made the world as a wilderness And destroyed its cities, Who did not open the house of his prisoners'?"*

After their rebellion, Lucifer became Satan (which means adversary or enemy) and his angels became demons (rebels). They are not empowered to harm mankind, *except by invitation*. It's not that difficult to understand; Satan counterfeits everything that God does. He knows that mankind has the sovereign right of freewill and he knows that he cannot impose his will on any human being. This is just the same with God, He does not impose His will on us. He will knock, inform and entreat, but no human being will ever be forcibly conscripted into the Kingdom of God.

Satan tempts us by appealing to our natural physical desires, our wants and needs. But he cannot compel us to sin, we do that of our own accord. Read **Genesis 3:1–7** If we continue down the path of sin, indulging in ever more lustful, selfish and hurtful deeds, God announces that he will give over such a person to their lusts, and consequently demonic domination. **Ro 1** *"²⁸And even as they did not like to retain God in their knowledge, God gave them over to a debased mind, to do those things which are not fitting;"* Once again, this is something that can be passed down to future generations.

So how can we tell the difference between a natural physical symptom, such as mental illness, or a deformity, and demon possession? The answer is, we can't by ourselves! Jesus was able to perceive which men or women had which problem and he granted that same gift of perception to his disciples. They were also given the authority to cast out those demons and we shall look at how that was done in

Personal Notes

Are you absolutely clear on the definition of sin, and Satan's part in all this? Do you understand how helpless humanity is without God? Have you grasped that, to one degree or another, every physical and mental defect relates back to your sinful condition. Pray for understanding and plead for wisdom.

Please be sure to look up the scriptures for yourself in your own Bible.

There is no healing without faith, no faith without the Word of God, no Word of God unless it lives within you by understanding and believing what it says.

Finish your notes on this chapter and get ready for even more revelation.

a later chapter. **Lk 10** *"¹⁹Behold, I give you the authority to trample on serpents and scorpions, and over all the power of the enemy, and nothing shall by any means hurt you. ²⁰Nevertheless do not rejoice in this, that the spirits are subject to you, but rather rejoice because your names are written in heaven."*

On the whole the church rarely teaches on this subject any more, probably for fear of ridicule. Unfortunately that ridicule can sometimes be justified when we see television images of religious people shouting and sweating, as they engage in a so-called "spiritual" battle to force a demon to leave someone. Sadly such shows make it difficult for anyone else trying to inform the church on this subject to be taken seriously. Consequently there are people around the world languishing in prisons and psychiatric institutions in need of this intervention, but with no-one to help them.

Some have asked whether Christians are susceptible to demonic possession. The short answer is no, but we can run the risk of exposure to demonic influence by not dealing with our fears. A biblical definition of fear is having faith and belief in something or someone who intends to harm you or those you care about. On the other hand, perfect love casts out fear and the source of perfect love is our heavenly Father. **1 Jn 4** *"¹⁸There is no fear in love; but perfect love casts out fear, because fear involves torment. But he who fears has not been made perfect in love. ¹⁹We love Him because He first loved us."* Our best defence against fear is faith, or the absolute conviction, that what God has promised to do for us He will do, and that means familiarising ourselves with the Word of God.

CHAPTER TWO

Are There Really Two Levels of Healing?

Not heard this one before? It's very simple: Jesus, His disciples and, later, some of the apostles healed people with just a few words. **Mt 8** "*16When evening had come, they brought to Him many who were demon-possessed. And He cast out the spirits with a word, and healed all who were sick,*"

Ac 5 "*12And through the hands of the apostles many signs and wonders were done among the people. And they were all with one accord in Solomon's Porch. 13Yet none of the rest dared join them, but the people esteemed them highly. 14And believers were increasingly added to the Lord, multitudes of both men and women, 15so that they brought the sick out into the streets and laid them on beds and couches, that at least the shadow of Peter passing by might fall on some of them. 16Also a multitude gathered from the surrounding cities to Jerusalem, bringing sick people and those who were tormented by unclean spirits, and they were all healed.*" Later on, we find the healing process has suddenly changed.

In **James 5:14**, the sick patient is advised to call for the elders of the church, so that they may pray over him, anointing him with oil in the name of the Lord. This is just one of several processes that afflicted Christians are required to go through. So what changed? None of the people Jesus and the first apostles healed had to go through this. For them, the healing was instantaneous.

You should consider the following and keep re-reading until you fully grasp the meaning behind it. During His entire time on earth our Saviour, Jesus Christ, never healed a single Christian. What's more, the stories documented of instantaneous healing by the disciples only ever happened to non-Christians. **Ac 3** *"¹Now Peter and John went up together to the temple at the hour of prayer, the ninth hour. ²And a certain man lame from his mother's womb was carried, whom they laid daily at the gate of the temple which is called Beautiful, to ask alms from those who entered the temple; ³who, seeing Peter and John about to go into the temple, asked for alms. ⁴And fixing his eyes on him, with John, Peter said, 'Look at us.' ⁵So he gave them his attention, expecting to receive something from them. ⁶Then Peter said, 'Silver and gold I do not have, but what I do have I give you: In the name of Jesus Christ of Nazareth, rise up and walk.' ⁷And he took him by the right hand and lifted him up, and immediately his feet and ankle bones received strength. ⁸So he, leaping up, stood and walked and entered the temple with them – walking, leaping, and praising God."* Is this true? Please check it for yourself. The successful deliverance for you or someone you care about hinges on your understanding and acceptance of this fact.

Now read that last paragraph again!

Can you now begin to see why the subject of healing has become such a divisive issue among so many different denominations within the church? There is virtually no agreement on what is required for a Christian to be healed.

But what is the proper definition of a Christian?

To answer this, and to take our subject further, the process of conversion must be clearly understood. At some point in their life a person may come to the realisation that they need "outside" help to deal with the pressures and difficulties of living. They may not even know anything about God, but something convicts them of the need to cry-out for that help. **Mt 7** *"⁸For everyone who asks receives, and he who seeks finds, and to him who knocks it will be opened."* **Lk 11** *"¹⁰For everyone who asks receives, and he who seeks finds, and to him who knocks*

Personal Notes

When you find out something new, it can be both exhilarating and nerve-wracking. No doubt questions are already occurring to you, which is good. Note down your questions on this page before you go any further. The answers will come as you progress through this book.

Do not forget to pray. Keep asking for wisdom and the treasures of heaven will be opened to you.

Are you unsure about what you have read? Take time to read through it again. Make sure you are reading all of the quoted scriptures in your own Bible.

it will be opened." Next, the person will receive a witness in some form that will be accompanied by a message about Jesus Christ. The door to their heart is being knocked upon and they cannot go any further without willingly responding to this "call".

Let us review this, because these points are crucial. A person initiates the conversion process because they are in a hopeless situation and can see no way out. Something in their own spirit tells them they should seek help from a yet-unknown source. God responds by bringing a witness which reveals the source of that help; so the ball is now back in our person's court. At this point they can now call upon the actual name of that source of help, believing that in doing so they will receive deliverance from their trouble.

Please note here, we are not yet talking about a fully converted, committed Christian who has been born again. At this stage, our seeker is responding to a witness given to him by Christ through one of His servants. If he believes that what has been witnessed to him can deliver him from his trouble, then he will be saved from that trouble because of his faith. **Joel 2** *"28And it shall come to pass That whoever calls on the name of the Lord Shall be saved. For in Mount Zion and in Jerusalem there shall be deliverance, As the Lord has said, Among the remnant whom the Lord calls."* That little faith is in itself a gift from God and can be attributed to the heartfelt prayers of existing believers who desire God's intervention in the life of non-believers, so everything is tied together as faith is always something given and received. It cannot be conjured-up by any personal effort, either on the part of the one in need or his known (or unknown) intercessor.

So the men and women, who were delivered from distress by Jesus during his earthly ministry, were aware of their helplessness. They were those who admitted, at least to themselves, that they needed outside help. Then they heard about, or actually saw, Jesus and then exercised the faith needed to ask Jesus directly for help; and in turn were rewarded for having the faith to believe that Jesus was able to help them through miraculous means.

24

Personal Notes

When you find out something new, it can be both exhilarating and nerve-wracking. No doubt questions are already occurring to you, which is good. Note down your questions on this page before you go any further. The answers will come as you progress through this book.

Do not forget to pray. Keep asking for wisdom and the treasures of heaven will be opened to you.

Are you unsure about what you have read? Take time to read through it again. Make sure you are reading all of the quoted scriptures in your own Bible.

Did all subsequently become Christians? Absolutely not. Some – such as nine of the ten healed lepers – couldn't even be bothered to thank Jesus for what He had done. **Lk 17** *"12Then as He entered a certain village, there met Him ten men who were lepers, who stood afar off. 13And they lifted up their voices and said, 'Jesus, Master, have mercy on us!' 14So when He saw them, He said to them, 'Go, show yourselves to the priests.' And so it was that as they went, they were cleansed. 15And one of them, when he saw that he was healed, returned, and with a loud voice glorified God, 16and fell down on his face at His feet, giving Him thanks. And he was a Samaritan. 17So Jesus answered and said, 'Were there not ten cleansed? But where are the nine? 18Were there not any found who returned to give glory to God except this foreigner?' 19And He said to him, 'Arise, go your way. Your faith has made you well'."*

So, initial faith and deliverance does not a Christian make. However, at the very least, it is still a powerful witness and should form as much a part of preaching the gospel today as it did during the ministry of Jesus Christ and the apostles.

Mk 5 *"18And when He got into the boat, he who had been demon-possessed begged Him that he might be with Him. 19However, Jesus did not permit him, but said to him, 'Go home to your friends, and tell them what great things the Lord has done for you, and how He has had compassion on you.' 20And he departed and began to proclaim in Decapolis all that Jesus had done for him; and all marvelled."*

Many are called but few are chosen! (**Matthew 22:14**) This scripture seems to imply that the choice of full conversion is not ours to make. Okay, consider this: How many of you, reading this book, chose to be born into this world? How many of you chose your parents or your siblings? How many of you chose the time and place of your birth? You played no part whatsoever in any of these decisions. You exist only because of the Sovereign will of your heavenly Father.

How much more then, do you suppose, is the importance attached to your spiritual birth. The timing is not yours to make. Every human being that has ever lived, is living now, or who will live in the future

Personal Notes

When you find out something new, it can be both exhilarating and nerve-wracking. No doubt questions are already occurring to you, which is good. Note down your questions on this page before you go any further. The answers will come as you progress through this book.

Do not forget to pray. Keep asking for wisdom and the treasures of heaven will be opened to you.

Are you unsure about what you have read? Take time to read through it again. Make sure you are reading all of the quoted scriptures in your own Bible.

has a predestined time for their call to a spiritual birth. **Ro 8** "*29For whom He foreknew, He also predestined to be conformed to the image of His Son, that He might be the firstborn among many brethren.*" It is the Father who has made that decision and He gives these new children over to Jesus Christ at the appropriate time. When that calling comes, it is irresistible. A living baby cannot resist being born into this physical life and the same applies to a spiritual babe in Christ. A "chosen one" can wrestle and struggle against this calling but he will know no peace until he accepts the inevitable nature of this calling.

So what about free will? What about the freedom of choice? Well, the answer lies in the question. No one can make an informed choice about something unless they're given all the facts. Let me use myself as an example. I was raised in a Christian household; yet I rebelled at the first opportunity so I could experience life for myself. There was much about the Christian life that I did not like. My parents' marriage seemed very unhappy, there seemed to be constant problems with finances and health, and certain doctrines of the church seemed unfair and grossly intolerant. So I went my own way. My prejudices against the church were reinforced as I learned more and more about the state of the world and I had no desire whatsoever to get "trapped" in this irrelevant religion.

As my life progressed I started to get into trouble, either through deliberate sin or force of circumstances. These were the only times that I chose to pray and ask for help and I always promised God that I would change if He would just help me out of this or that situation. This happened nearly a dozen times. Each time He forgave and delivered me from that present distress, and each time I failed utterly to live up to my promises. I was confused. Why was God so willing to help me whenever I asked? Wouldn't He be perfectly justified to refuse to help because of my faithless and rebellious attitude and lifestyle? I didn't know it then but He was laying the groundwork for our future relationship. I felt so guilty and unhappy because I felt I was letting Him down all the time and I had a desire to please Him and make it up to Him. But, of course I couldn't do it. I was still

Personal Notes

When you find out something new, it can be both exhilarating and nerve-wracking. No doubt questions are already occurring to you, which is good. Note down your questions on this page before you go any further. The answers will come as you progress through this book.

Do not forget to pray. Keep asking for wisdom and the treasures of heaven will be opened to you.

Are you unsure about what you have read? Take time to read through it again. Make sure you are reading all of the quoted scriptures in your own Bible.

steeped in sin, and, of course, those nagging questions about the Christian faith just wouldn't go away.

Having established the groundwork, however, God began to deal with the questions. One by one He stripped away every excuse I had for not committing to Him, until I had no excuses left. He revealed a great deal to me to answer my questions but in my smugness at knowing so much, I thought there was a way out and I could still walk away. **Ro 11** *"29For the gifts and the calling of God are irrevocable."* Big mistake! Suddenly my world was in a complete turmoil. Everything that could go wrong went wrong. I was oppressed on every side and in less than a month after making that fateful decision, I had lost a very promising career in the most unbelievable of circumstances. There was not the tiniest hint of doubt in my mind about what had happened. I knew too much, there was no way out and so I finally capitulated. I surrendered and in that moment, for the first time in my life, a peace came upon me that I had never known before and since that day I have never looked back.

Do you really think that the Apostle Paul had any choice in his calling? See **Acts:9**.

Each of us is brought to a point of decision and the final decision is ours to make; but for every believer it will be a decision based on full knowledge, anything less cannot be valid.

It was six months after I surrendered whole-heartedly to God that I finally had enough counselling, understanding and had begun to show the fruits of repentance: (**Lk 3** *"8Therefore bear fruits worthy of repentance, 10So the people asked him, saying, 'What shall we do then?' 11He answered and said to them, 'He who has two tunics, let him give to him who has none; and he who has food, let him do likewise.' 12Then tax collectors also came to be baptized, and said to him, 'Teacher, what shall we do?' 13And he said to them, 'Collect no more than what is appointed for you.' 14Likewise the soldiers asked him, saying, 'And what shall we do?' So he said to them, 'Do not intimidate anyone or accuse falsely, and be content with your wages'."*) that I could take the final step of baptism and

Personal Notes

When you find out something new, it can be both exhilarating and nerve-wracking. No doubt questions are already occurring to you, which is good. Note down your questions on this page before you go any further. The answers will come as you progress through this book.

Do not forget to pray. Keep asking for wisdom and the treasures of heaven will be opened to you.

Are you unsure about what you have read? Take time to read through it again. Make sure you are reading all of the quoted scriptures in your own Bible.

receive the laying on of hands to receive the Holy Spirit. It was a carefully considered decision, one in which I was aware of all the possible consequences as well as the blessings. But ultimately it was my decision, though, for me, it was an easy one to make.

Repentance and faith are gifts from God; we cannot earn them. **Ro 3** *"24being justified freely by His grace through the redemption that is in Christ Jesus."* From the point we accept Jesus Christ as our personal saviour, we accept His sacrifice as an atonement for our sinful ways. In faith we believe that we have been reconciled to the Father by grace. If we sin in the future, we know that we have a blood covenant with the Father that, so long as we confess our sins and seek His forgiveness, He will faithfully forgive us as He has promised to do under the new covenant.

Under the terms of the new covenant to which all blood-bought believers are signed up, our Father commits Himself to do many things for us. **Heb 9** *"15And for this reason He is the Mediator of the new covenant, by means of death, for the redemption of the transgressions under the first covenant, that those who are called may receive the promise of the eternal inheritance."* Our eternal future is secure, we cannot be more saved than we already are. Jesus Christ has paid that debt for us. Now it's time to discuss our obligations under the terms of the new covenant. This is where we demonstrate our faith by our works. **Tit 2** *"7in all things showing yourself to be a pattern of good works; in doctrine showing integrity, reverence, incorruptibility, 8sound speech that cannot be condemned, that one who is an opponent may be ashamed, having nothing evil to say of you."* These works do not make us any more saved, but they do make a significant difference to the remainder of our physical lives and those of our families, especially in the area of physical healing.

CHAPTER THREE

Did Jesus Make a Huge Mistake, Or Have We?

That question sounds almost blasphemous doesn't it? Yet, the church appears to have made certain assumptions that cause contradictions in different parts of the Bible. This is wisdom: By amazing, miraculous means, the Creator of heaven and earth has made sure that the Bible is complete in its present form, that nothing was lost in the translation and the Bible does not contradict itself. **2 Ti 3** *"16All Scripture is given by inspiration of God, and is profitable for doctrine, for reproof, for correction, for instruction in righteousness."* Once you realise and accept this, you cannot be led astray by erroneous interpretations of scripture. In other words, if it appears that one scripture is contradicting another, or seems to be making God out to be unfair and unjust, then you can be certain that the error is in your understanding or in that of your teacher.

We are now going to look at a critical area of the Bible that has been misjudged, misrepresented and misinterpreted. Please now read chapters fourteen to seventeen in the Book of John.

It would be fair to say that within these four critical chapters lies the entire basis of the new covenant. Namely the very nature of our personal and corporate relationship with God. This can be summarised in **John 13** *"34A new commandment I give to you, that you love one another; as I have loved you, that you also love one another. 35By this all will know that you are My disciples, if you have love for one another."* In the context of our present time, Jesus is talking about our relationship with hundreds of thousands, if not millions, of other believers. **Jn 17** *"20I do not pray for these alone, but also for those who will believe in Me through their word; 21that they all may be one, as You, Father, are in Me, and I in You; that they also may be one in Us, that the world may believe that You sent Me."* Do we express the love of God in our thoughts, words and actions to all believers we come across regardless of their denomination or are we judgemental, superior and uncaring? Notice the predominant theme in those four following chapters: "If you love me, keep my commandments!" repeated in at least six verses.

At the time of our conversion, we were assured of eternal life and made sinless by grace. On the strength of that alone, we could have shed our mortal life and gone home to be with Christ. This is vitally important to understand. If you have ever been a parent, you know that you go to great lengths to prepare your home for the arrival of your new child, all your energies and resources are expended toward that goal. Once the baby has been delivered, what do you do? You bring your child home where he will be ensconced in the safety and comfort of your house and will be loved and cared for there.

Jesus said, *"Father I ask not that you take them out of this world, but leave them in the world."* **Jn 17:15** The fact that Jesus is asking the Father to permit His children to be left in the world suggests that the desire of the Father is to bring His new children home where they cannot be harmed and where they will be safe and cared for. Instead, both the Father and Jesus Christ are in perfect agreement that we should be left in the world but with significant protection and provision until such time as each of our life purposes has been completed.

Please understand, there is nothing that you can do that will make you more saved than you already are. Eternal life is assured. **Lk 12** *"32Do not fear, little flock, for it is your Father's good pleasure to give you the kingdom,"* and we are living in the presence of God, each of us with our own divinely assigned angel to watch over us. **Heb 1** *"14Are they not all ministering spirits sent forth to minister for those who will inherit salvation?"*

Personal Notes

If you know to do good, yet do not do it, to you – it then becomes sin (**James 4:17**). Review what God has told you so far. Do not despair if you find numerous areas in your life that need changing; you cannot do it all at once and you will certainly fail if you try to do it on your own strength.

Place every situation before God. Acknowledge your sin and humble yourself before Him and He will set you back on the road to recovery. You are no different from anyone else. We all have to go through this. Your deliverance is getting closer. Stay the course and continue to work through this book.

So why are we called upon to grow in faith and knowledge? **2 Pe 3** *"18but grow in the grace and knowledge of our Lord and Saviour Jesus Christ. To Him be the glory both now and forever."* Well it is not to improve on the security of our salvation. No, we are trained up for an earthly purpose, to take up our rightful place in the "great commission". That is now the sole purpose of our lives in everything we think, say and do. Our personal lives are to be a witness to this world. For example, if you are married, then your conduct within marriage in full compliance with God's marital laws will be a living witness to how fantastic that relationship can be. So you will be a light to the world, and unbelievers will be attracted to that example and will ask you about it and then you confirm that witness through your personal testimony of how your Father has made this possible.

A similar thing applies if you are a parent, employer, employee or as a neighbour, and especially concerning your relationship with your spiritual brothers and sisters. **Eph 5** *"1Therefore be imitators of God as dear children. 2And walk in love, as Christ also has loved us and given Himself for us, an offering and a sacrifice to God for a sweet-smelling aroma. 3But fornication and all uncleanness or covetousness, let it not even be named among you, as is fitting for saints; 4neither filthiness, nor foolish talking, nor coarse jesting, which are not fitting, but rather giving of thanks. 8For you were once darkness, but now you are light in the Lord. Walk as children of light 9(for the fruit of the Spirit is in all goodness, righteousness, and truth), 10finding out what is acceptable to the Lord. 17Therefore do not be unwise, but understand what the will of the Lord is. 18And do not be drunk with wine, in which is dissipation; but be filled with the Spirit, 19speaking to one another in psalms and hymns and spiritual songs, singing and making melody in your heart to the Lord, 20giving thanks always for all things to God the Father in the name of our Lord Jesus Christ, 21submitting to one another in the fear of God. 23For the husband is head of the wife, as also Christ is head of the church; and He is the Saviour of the body. 24Therefore, just as the church is subject to Christ, so let the wives be to their own husbands in everything. 25Husbands, love your wives, just as Christ also loved the church and gave Himself for her, 26that He might sanctify and cleanse her with the washing of water by the word, 27that He might present her to Himself a glorious church, not having spot or wrinkle or any such*

Personal Notes

If you know to do good, yet do not do it, to you – it then becomes sin (**James 4:17**). Review what God has told you so far. Do not despair if you find numerous areas in your life that need changing; you cannot do it all at once and you will certainly fail if you try to do it on your own strength.

Place every situation before God. Acknowledge your sin and humble yourself before Him and He will set you back on the road to recovery. You are no different from anyone else. We all have to go through this. Your deliverance is getting closer. Stay the course and continue to work through this book.

thing, but that she should be holy and without blemish. 28So husbands ought to love their own wives as their own bodies; he who loves his wife loves himself. 29For no one ever hated his own flesh, but nourishes and cherishes it, just as the Lord does the church. 30For we are members of His body, of His flesh and of His bones. 33Nevertheless let each one of you in particular so love his own wife as himself, and let the wife see that she respects her husband." **Eph 6** *"4And you, fathers, do not provoke your children to wrath, but bring them up in the training and admonition of the Lord. 5Bondservants, be obedient to those who are your masters according to the flesh, with fear and trembling, in sincerity of heart, as to Christ; 6not with eyeservice, as men-pleasers, but as bondservants of Christ, doing the will of God from the heart, 7with goodwill doing service, as to the Lord, and not to men, 8knowing that whatever good anyone does, he will receive the same from the Lord, whether he is a slave or free. 9And you, masters, do the same things to them, giving up threatening, knowing that your own Master also is in heaven, and there is no partiality with Him."*

What has all this got to do with healing? Everything. As Christians, illness should not be afflicting us, we should not be struggling in poverty. If something is going badly wrong with any aspect of our personal lives, then we should take a close look at our personal commitment to the great commission. If we are failing in our example, then we must repent and seek the strength to change. If we are failing to support, both in prayer and finances, an existing evangelistic ministry then we should repent and immediately submit a substantial offering and pray daily for the unconverted to be reached through this ministry. **2 Co 9** *"1Now concerning the ministering to the saints, it is superfluous for me to write to you; 6But this I say: He who sows sparingly will also reap sparingly, and he who sows bountifully will also reap bountifully. 7So let each one give as he purposes in his heart, not grudgingly or of necessity; for God loves a cheerful giver. 8And God is able to make all grace abound toward you, that you, always having all sufficiency in all things, may have an abundance for every good work. 9As it is written: 'He has dispersed abroad, He has given to the poor; His righteousness endures forever.' 10Now may He who supplies seed to the sower, and bread for food, supply and multiply the seed you have sown and increase the fruits of your righteousness, 11while you are enriched in everything for all*

Personal Notes

If you know to do good, yet do not do it, to you – it then becomes sin (**James 4:17**). Review what God has told you so far. Do not despair if you find numerous areas in your life that need changing; you cannot do it all at once and you will certainly fail if you try to do it on your own strength.

Place every situation before God. Acknowledge your sin and humble yourself before Him and He will set you back on the road to recovery. You are no different from anyone else. We all have to go through this. Your deliverance is getting closer. Stay the course and continue to work through this book.

liberality, which causes thanksgiving through us to God. ¹²For the admin-istration of this service not only supplies the needs of the saints, but also is abounding through many thanksgivings to God, ¹³while, through the proof of this ministry, they glorify God for the obedience of your confession to the gospel of Christ, and for your liberal sharing with them and all men, ¹⁴and by their prayer for you, who long for you because of the exceeding grace of God in you."

Are you actively seeking a personal role to play in the great com-mission but are unsure of your talents, or your personal circumstances just don't seem right, so you end up doing nothing? All such concerns must be placed before the Father and while you wait for the revealing of that future role, commit yourself to stay faithful in the smaller things so that you can be trusted over much. **Mt 25** *"²¹His lord said to him, 'Well done, good and faithful servant; you were faithful over a few things, I will make you ruler over many things. Enter into the joy of your lord'."*

We must bear fruit for the Kingdom of God. God's love in us must bear fruit by our obedience to fulfil our part in the great commission so that others will receive a powerful witness, and perhaps be saved if this is their time. If we are not bearing fruit, we are in trouble and quite often that will be physically manifested in illness, or financial or relational problems.

Mt 25 *"¹⁴For the kingdom of heaven is like a man travelling to a far coun-try, who called his own servants and delivered his goods to them. ¹⁵And to one he gave five talents, to another two, and to another one, to each accord-ing to his own ability; and immediately he went on a journey. ¹⁹After a long time the lord of those servants came and settled accounts with them. ²⁰So he who had received five talents came and brought five other talents, saying, 'Lord, you delivered to me five talents; look, I have gained five more talents besides them.' ²¹His lord said to him, 'Well done, good and faithful servant; you were faithful over a few things, I will make you ruler over many things. Enter into the joy of your lord.' ²²He also who had received two talents came and said, 'Lord, you delivered to me two talents; look, I have gained two more talents besides them.' ²³His lord said to him, 'Well done, good and*

Personal Notes

If you know to do good, yet do not do it, to you – it then becomes sin (**James 4:17**). Review what God has told you so far. Do not despair if you find numerous areas in your life that need changing; you cannot do it all at once and you will certainly fail if you try to do it on your own strength.

Place every situation before God. Acknowledge your sin and humble yourself before Him and He will set you back on the road to recovery. You are no different from anyone else. We all have to go through this. Your deliverance is getting closer. Stay the course and continue to work through this book.

faithful servant; you have been faithful over a few things, I will make you ruler over many things. Enter into the joy of your lord.' 24*Then he who had received the one talent came and said, 'Lord, I knew you to be a hard man, reaping where you have not sown, and gathering where you have not scattered seed.* 25*And I was afraid, and went and hid your talent in the ground. Look, there you have what is yours.'* 26*But his lord answered and said to him, 'You wicked and lazy servant, you knew that I reap where I have not sown, and gather where I have not scattered seed.* 27*So you ought to have deposited my money with the bankers,* [supported an existing ministry] *and at my coming I would have received back my own with interest.* 28*Therefore take the talent from him, and give it to him who has ten talents.* 29*For to everyone who has, more will be given, and he will have abundance; but from him who does not have, even what he has will be taken away.* 30*And cast the unprofitable servant into the outer darkness. There will be weeping and gnashing of teeth'."* [not eternal judgement, but major personal difficulties]

If there is a failure to repent of this unfruitful, lazy attitude, the final consequence will be as follows: **Mt 25** "31*When the Son of Man comes in His glory, and all the holy angels with Him, then He will sit on the throne of His glory.* 32*All the nations will be gathered before Him, and He will separate them one from another, as a shepherd divides his sheep from the goats.* 33*And He will set the sheep on His right hand, but the goats on the left.* 34*Then the King will say to those on His right hand, 'Come, you blessed of My Father, inherit the kingdom prepared for you from the foundation of the world:* 35*for I was hungry and you gave Me food; I was thirsty and you gave Me drink; I was a stranger and you took Me in;* 36*I was naked and you clothed Me; I was sick and you visited Me; I was in prison and you came to Me.'* 37*Then the righteous will answer Him, saying, 'Lord, when did we see You hungry and feed You, or thirsty and give You drink?* 38*When did we see You a stranger and take You in, or naked and clothe You?* 39*Or when did we see You sick, or in prison, and come to You?'* 40*And the King will answer and say to them, 'Assuredly, I say to you, inasmuch as you did it to one of the least of these My brethren, you did it to Me.'* 41*Then He will also say to those on the left hand, 'Depart from Me, you cursed, into the everlasting fire prepared for the devil and his angels:* 42*for I was hungry and you gave Me no food; I was thirsty and you gave Me no drink;* 43*I was a stranger and you*

Personal Notes

If you know to do good, yet do not do it, to you – it then becomes sin (**James 4:17**). Review what God has told you so far. Do not despair if you find numerous areas in your life that need changing; you cannot do it all at once and you will certainly fail if you try to do it on your own strength.

Place every situation before God. Acknowledge your sin and humble yourself before Him and He will set you back on the road to recovery. You are no different from anyone else. We all have to go through this. Your deliverance is getting closer. Stay the course and continue to work through this book.

did not take Me in, naked and you did not clothe Me, sick and in prison and you did not visit Me.' ⁴⁴*Then they also will answer Him, saying, 'Lord, when did we see You hungry or thirsty or a stranger or naked or sick or in prison, and did not minister to You?'* ⁴⁵*Then He will answer them, saying, 'Assuredly, I say to you, inasmuch as you did not do it to one of the least of these, you did not do it to Me.'* ⁴⁶*And these will go away into everlasting punishment, but the righteous into eternal life."*

Mt 7 *"²¹Not everyone who says to Me, 'Lord, Lord,' shall enter the kingdom of heaven, but he who does the will of My Father in heaven."*

None of the strength, wisdom, gifts and growth you need to carry out your part in the great commission is available to you naturally. You must constantly seek all these things from your Father who gives you both the will and the means to carry out His work. Anyone who tries to do these things by their own strength is doomed to fail. We sow and we water but it is God who gives the increase.

Anyone who loves their present physical life or, put another way, anyone who fears death does not possess the fulness of God's love. **Mk 8** *"³⁵For whoever desires to save his life will lose it, but whoever loses his life for My sake and the gospel's will save it."* This will automatically interfere with that believer's ability to obey God when called to go into potentially hazardous situations. **Heb 10** *"³⁸Now the just shall live by faith; But if anyone draws back, My soul has no pleasure in him."*

Lk 14 *"²⁶If anyone comes to Me and does not hate* (or love less by comparison) *his father and mother, wife and children, brothers and sisters, yes, and his own life also, he cannot be My disciple."* Abraham adored his son as did his wife Sarah, but God commanded him to sacrifice his son. If this was required of Abraham, what might be required of us? Paul says in **1 Corinthians 2:9** *"eye has not seen nor ear heard what God has prepared for those who love him."* God describes himself as a jealous god and will not accept idolatry which is the worship of the created rather than the creator. Where does your priority lie? If God is not at the head of your life regarding everything and anything, then there is potential idolatry. The kingdom of God must come first, we were

Personal Notes

If you know to do good, yet do not do it, to you – it then becomes sin (**James 4:17**). Review what God has told you so far. Do not despair if you find numerous areas in your life that need changing; you cannot do it all at once and you will certainly fail if you try to do it on your own strength.

Place every situation before God. Acknowledge your sin and humble yourself before Him and He will set you back on the road to recovery. You are no different from anyone else. We all have to go through this. Your deliverance is getting closer. Stay the course and continue to work through this book.

bought with a great price, so we must be faithful by fulfilling everything we've been called to do.

God is willing to heal all who come to him. **Jas 3** *"¹⁷But the wisdom that is from above is first pure, then peaceable, gentle, willing to yield, full of mercy and good fruits, without partiality and without hypocrisy."* By his stripes we are healed! **1 Pe 2** *"²⁴who Himself bore our sins in His own body on the tree, that we, having died to sins, might live for righteousness – by whose stripes you were healed."* It's already happened, the only obstacle to receiving healing is us!

Putting the kingdom of God first with regard to our personal responsibility to fulfil the great commission is an essential part of our christian lives. Carry out the test contained in all the scriptures quoted in this chapter by answering the questions contained within them. If you are deficient in any of these areas, confess them before your Father, accept His forgiveness and immediately move to correct them.

The message contained in the four chapters of **John** are very much for us today and must be read in that context. As you progress through this book, everything that stands in the way of your deliverance will be shown and revealed. How you respond will determine the outcome of the rest of your life. **Jas 4** *"⁸Draw near to God and He will draw near to you. Cleanse your hands, you sinners; and purify your hearts, you double-minded. ⁹Lament and mourn and weep! Let your laughter be turned to mourning and your joy to gloom. ¹⁰Humble yourselves in the sight of the Lord, and He will lift you up."*

Before we leave this chapter, let us deal with one more scripture that has been used wrongly to justify acceptance of physical and mental distress: **2 Co 12** *"⁷And lest I should be exalted above measure by the abundance of the revelations, a thorn in the flesh was given to me, a messenger of Satan to buffet me, lest I be exalted above measure. ⁸Concerning this thing I pleaded with the Lord three times that it might depart from me. ⁹And He said to me, 'My grace is sufficient for you, for My strength is made perfect in weakness.' Therefore most gladly I will rather boast in my infirmities, that the power of Christ may rest upon me. ¹⁰Therefore I take pleasure in*

Personal Notes

If you know to do good, yet do not do it, to you – it then becomes sin (**James 4:17**). Review what God has told you so far. Do not despair if you find numerous areas in your life that need changing; you cannot do it all at once and you will certainly fail if you try to do it on your own strength.

Place every situation before God. Acknowledge your sin and humble yourself before Him and He will set you back on the road to recovery. You are no different from anyone else. We all have to go through this. Your deliverance is getting closer. Stay the course and continue to work through this book.

infirmities, in reproaches, in needs, in persecutions, in distresses, for Christ's sake. For when I am weak, then I am strong."

Many teachers argue that Paul was referring to a sickness or disability but that has no basis in truth. The following context explains everything: **Ro 7** *"[14]For we know that the law is spiritual, but I am carnal, sold under sin. [15]For what I am doing, I do not understand. For what I will to do, that I do not practice; but what I hate, that I do. [16]If, then, I do what I will not to do, I agree with the law that it is good. [17]But now, it is no longer I who do it, but sin that dwells in me. [18]For I know that in me (that is, in my flesh) nothing good dwells; for to will is present with me, but how to perform what is good I do not find. [19]For the good that I will to do, I do not do; but the evil I will not to do, that I practice. [20]Now if I do what I will not to do, it is no longer I who do it, but sin that dwells in me. [21]I find then a law, that evil is present with me, the one who wills to do good. [22]For I delight in the law of God according to the inward man. [23]But I see another law in my members, warring against the law of my mind, and bringing me into captivity to the law of sin which is in my members. [24]O wretched man that I am! Who will deliver me from this body of death? [25]I thank God — through Jesus Christ our Lord! So then, with the mind I myself serve the law of God, but with the flesh the law of sin."*

Paul was dealing with a personal sin. What it was is none of our business. He prayed three times to be delivered from this weakness but Jesus told him that His grace would cover him. Was this giving Paul permission to continue in this sin? Absolutely not, but his struggle would help to retain his humility and keep him ever reliant upon God.

You do not need grace to remain sick or disabled. There are plenty of unbelievers in that situation. For instance, some believers struggle with sexual sin and lean on Christ day by day to hold that temptation at bay. Others are permanently delivered, or never had that weakness to begin with.

CHAPTER FOUR

My Church Group Makes Me Sick!

Every church is made up of individuals with varying gifts, backgrounds, opinions and different levels of growth. This is a potentially combustible mix. So much variety, so many differences, yet we have the same Father, the same Saviour and the same Spirit.

Ro 6 *"5For if we have been united together in the likeness of His death, certainly we also shall be in the likeness of His resurrection,"* God describes us as His family and he has set each member in the Body of Christ as it has pleased Him. **Eph 4** *"1I, therefore, the prisoner of the Lord, beseech you to walk worthy of the calling with which you were called, 2with all lowliness and gentleness, with longsuffering, bearing with one another in love, 3endeavouring to keep the unity of the Spirit in the bond of peace. 4There is one body and one Spirit, just as you were called in one hope of your calling; 5one Lord, one faith, one baptism; 6one God and Father of all, who is above all, and through all, and in you all. 7But to each one of us grace was given according to the measure of Christ's gift. 11And He Himself gave some to be apostles, some prophets, some evangelists, and some pastors and teachers, 12for the equipping of the saints for the work of ministry, for the edifying of the body of Christ, 13till we all come to the unity of the faith and of the knowledge of the Son of God, to a perfect man, to the measure of the stature of the fullness of Christ; 14that we should no longer be children, tossed to and fro and carried about with every wind of doctrine, by the trickery of men, in the cunning craftiness of deceitful plotting, 15but, speaking the truth in love, may grow up in all things into Him who is the head – Christ – 16from whom the whole body, joined and knit together by what every joint* *supplies, according to the effective working by which every part does its share, causes growth of the body for the edifying of itself in love."*

Unity will never prevail in the Church without humility among its members, with each one esteeming the other as being better than himself. **Php 2** *"³Let nothing be done through selfish ambition or conceit, but in lowliness of mind let each esteem others better than himself."* It's very easy to write this and very easy for you to read this, but it's quite another thing to actually live it. We cannot accomplish this by ourselves, we need Godly love within us before we can actively practise this among others. So it all comes back to the state of our personal relationship with God. If He is first in our lives, if we communicate with Him on a daily basis and familiarise ourselves with His Word and seek to obey Him in everything then the ability to love our fellow man will become so much easier than trying to do it in our own strength.

1 Co 13 *"¹Though I speak with the tongues of men and of angels, but have not love, I have become sounding brass or a clanging cymbal. ²And though I have the gift of prophecy, and understand all mysteries and all knowledge, and though I have all faith, so that I could remove mountains, but have not love, I am nothing. ³And though I bestow all my goods to feed the poor, and though I give my body to be burned, but have not love, it profits me nothing. ⁴Love suffers long and is kind; love does not envy; love does not parade itself, is not puffed up; ⁵does not behave rudely, does not seek its own, is not provoked, thinks no evil; ⁶does not rejoice in iniquity, but rejoices in the truth; ⁷bears all things, believes all things, hopes all things, endures all things."*

Within your own congregation, you will have members with different strengths and weaknesses. For instance, I am not addicted to alcohol. Never have been. Never will be. I see the destructive effects of this addiction on personal health, the family and on society. In the UK no social event appears complete without the liberal supply of alcohol. I hate what this is doing to our country and I rage inwardly at the complacency of our leaders in not roundly condemning such destructive behaviour and not taking what, to me, would be obvious steps to deal with it. But my ability to empathise with those who

Personal Notes

When the people of the world see the church, they need to see unity, love, peace, joy in order to be filled with a desire to be part of it. Instead they see factions, in-fighting, put-downs – you name it – and so the world stays away.

As a journey begins with one step, so the attitude of a small or large group begins with one good example. Make notes of what the Holy Spirit is telling you to do to be such an example and commit yourself to be a light for Christ in this crucial area.

struggle with this addiction is impaired by my lack of personal experience in this area. Therefore, the temptation to be judgemental and lack compassion for those so afflicted is very real. So, how do I deal with that?

First, I look at my own weak areas – and there are more than one. **Lk 6** *"37Judge not, and you shall not be judged. Condemn not, and you shall not be condemned. Forgive, and you will be forgiven. 41And why do you look at the speck in your brother's eye, but do not perceive the plank in your own eye? 42Or how can you say to your brother, 'Brother, let me remove the speck that is in your eye,' when you yourself do not see the plank that is in your own eye? Hypocrite! First remove the plank from your own eye, and then you will see clearly to remove the speck that is in your brother's eye."* I look at how many times I have slipped up, sometimes causing offence to others. Then I look at the incredible patience and grace of God who refuses to condemn me when I repent. He constantly sets the example of perfect love and then urges me to go and do likewise. He reminds me of how much I need Him to provide supernatural strength in the areas where I do not possess it naturally. Then He confronts me with my deeply held prejudices, suspicions and the fear that emanates from that. (*See* Chapter 6 Who are your Ninevites?)

God chooses the weak and foolish of the world to make up His family. **1 Co 1** *"27But God has chosen the foolish things of the world to put to shame the wise, and God has chosen the weak things of the world to put to shame the things which are mighty;"* Hardly something for us to boast about and yet, surprisingly, there are many in the Church today who seem to view themselves as being better than the unbelievers by virtue of their calling. Jesus Christ never had that attitude. He associated himself with the humble, the despised, the outcasts. Who do you go and speak to after services? Do you seek out the quiet ones who are difficult to talk to? Do you open your home to the singles and the elderly? Are you always first in the queue to offer a ride to those without transport, even when it takes you miles out of your way? Do you go to every church meeting with only one thing in mind: "How can I be a blessing to my brothers and sisters today?" If

Personal Notes

When the people of the world see the church, they need to see unity, love, peace, joy in order to be filled with a desire to be part of it. Instead they see factions, in-fighting, put-downs – you name it – and so the world stays away.

As a journey begins with one step, so the attitude of a small or large group begins with one good example. Make notes of what the Holy Spirit is telling you to do to be such an example and commit yourself to be a light for Christ in this crucial area.

that is your attitude concerning your local church then you have Christ and you are bearing fruit for his kingdom.

Here is wisdom. No matter where you go, you won't find any church of any denomination that has perfect love, perfect truth or perfect leadership and it's all God's "fault". Why? Because He chose to work with human beings. He didn't have to; he could have raised up stones to do His work and had a lot less hassle.

You could ask, "Well what about the original twelve apostles, weren't they perfect?" Far from it. Each man, just as the church today, had different strengths, weaknesses, gifts and personalities. But they were close to Jesus and they loved him. Their unity resulted from their shared love of their saviour. So where's that unity today?

In any one town across the UK you can find half-a-dozen or more different denominations represented in your area: Baptist, Pentecostal, Catholic, Church of England, Methodist, Salvation Army, Church of God, to name just some.

They all proclaim the name of Christ, their most basic doctrines are broadly the same and they all, without exception, have more than their fair share of health, financial and relationship problems. Many of them have something else in common too, a blind refusal to work and cooperate with each other concerning the work of God in your community. Why?

Many reasons will be given, but it can all be distilled down to fear and suspicion. Satan has no reason to be concerned about a divided Church. **Mt 12** *"25Every kingdom divided against itself is brought to desolation, and every city or house divided against itself will not stand."*

Most church services have an announcement period calling upon their local members to pray for those afflicted among them. How often do you hear of that period being used for afflicted members of another denomination? When was the last time your church group took up a generous offering for another group? When were they last

Personal Notes

When the people of the world see the church, they need to see unity, love, peace, joy in order to be filled with a desire to be part of it. Instead they see factions, in-fighting, put-downs – you name it – and so the world stays away.

As a journey begins with one step, so the attitude of a small or large group begins with one good example. Make notes of what the Holy Spirit is telling you to do to be such an example and commit yourself to be a light for Christ in this crucial area.

invited to an event that you were hosting? Most importantly, what does our Father think of all this? **Ro 12** *"[1]I beseech you therefore, brethren, by the mercies of God, that you present your bodies as a living sacrifice, holy, acceptable to God, which is your reasonable service. [2]And do not be conformed to this world, but be transformed by the renewing of your mind, that you may prove what is that good and acceptable and perfect will of God. [3]For I say, through the grace given to me, to everyone who is among you, not to think of himself more highly than he ought to think, but to think soberly, as God has dealt to each one a measure of faith. [4]For as we have many members in one body, but all the members do not have the same function, [5]so we, being many, are one body in Christ, and individually members of one another. [6]Having then gifts differing according to the grace that is given to us, let us use them: if prophecy, let us prophesy in proportion to our faith; [7]or ministry, let us use it in our ministering; he who teaches, in teaching; [8]he who exhorts, in exhortation; he who gives, with liberality; he who leads, with diligence; he who shows mercy, with cheerfulness. [9]Let love be without hypocrisy. Abhor what is evil. Cling to what is good. [10]Be kindly affectionate to one another with brotherly love, in honor giving preference to one another; [11]not lagging in diligence, fervent in spirit, serving the Lord; [12]rejoicing in hope, patient in tribulation, continuing steadfastly in prayer; [13]distributing to the needs of the saints, given to hospitality. [14]Bless those who persecute you; bless and do not curse. [15]Rejoice with those who rejoice, and weep with those who weep. [16]Be of the same mind toward one another. Do not set your mind on high things, but associate with the humble. Do not be wise in your own opinion. [17]Repay no one evil for evil. Have regard for good things in the sight of all men. [18]If it is possible, as much as depends on you, live peaceably with all men."*

We live in a selfish generation. Some of that attitude has permeated through to our churches. Be in no doubt; we are living in the last days as prophesied by Christ **2 Ti 3** *"[1]But know this, that in the last days perilous times will come: [2]For men will be lovers of themselves, lovers of money, boasters, proud, blasphemers, disobedient to parents, unthankful, unholy, [3]unloving, unforgiving, slanderers, without self-control, brutal, despisers of good, [4]traitors, headstrong, haughty, lovers of pleasure rather than lovers of God, [5]having a form of godliness but denying its power. And from such people turn away! [6]For of this sort are those who creep into households and*

Personal Notes

When the people of the world see the church, they need to see unity, love, peace, joy in order to be filled with a desire to be part of it. Instead they see factions, in-fighting, put-downs – you name it – and so the world stays away.

As a journey begins with one step, so the attitude of a small or large group begins with one good example. Make notes of what the Holy Spirit is telling you to do to be such an example and commit yourself to be a light for Christ in this crucial area.

make captives of gullible women loaded down with sins, led away by various lusts, ⁷always learning and never able to come to the knowledge of the truth. ⁸Now as Jannes and Jambres resisted Moses, so do these also resist the truth: men of corrupt minds, disapproved concerning the faith; ⁹but they will progress no further, for their folly will be manifest to all, as theirs also was." and the very unity, needed to complete the witness of the gospel to the ends of the earth, presently eludes the Church. **1 Co 1** *"¹⁰Now I plead with you, brethren, by the name of our Lord Jesus Christ, that you all speak the same thing, and that there be no divisions among you, but that you be perfectly joined together in the same mind and in the same judgement."* If we don't repent and begin to co-operate on a scale never, ever, seen before we will be bypassed and God will recruit from a different pool of believers. **Mt 22** *"⁸Then he said to his servants, 'The wedding is ready, but those who were invited were not worthy. ⁹Therefore go into the highways, and as many as you find, invite to the wedding'."*

Repentance in this crucial area would also bring with it supernatural favour, healings and great and abundant blessings. When Paul was asked by the Corinthian church (**1 Corinthinans 11**) why so many of them were getting sick and not being healed, he responded by talking about something that frankly does not make much sense, until you see it in context. Paul begins by castigating the Corinthian church for the slovenly way in which they were observing the Lord's supper, selfishly consuming the bread, unwilling to wait for the others. Eating and drinking to satisfy human appetites as opposed to the solemn manner dictated by such a sombre and important occasion.

He reaffirms the symbolic nature of such an occasion by reminding the Corinthians that the pieces of bread represents the Body of Christ (the church) and the wine, his spilled blood, symbolising the new covenant. There was an attitude of selfishness and one-upmanship present, in which the poorer members were looked down upon (other denominations?). In verse **29** we then come to a strange scripture which when first read appears to be self-explanatory, but which contains a much deeper significance.

Personal Notes

When the people of the world see the church, they need to see unity, love, peace, joy in order to be filled with a desire to be part of it. Instead they see factions, in-fighting, put-downs – you name it – and so the world stays away.

As a journey begins with one step, so the attitude of a small or large group begins with one good example. Make notes of what the Holy Spirit is telling you to do to be such an example and commit yourself to be a light for Christ in this crucial area.

The usual explanation for this verse is that an unworthy participant in the Lord's supper does not fully comprehend the magnitude of the sacrifice that Jesus made for him personally. This is accurate to a point, but the deeper meaning concerns the whole church. What Jesus did, He did for the whole church, for all the members. I don't represent the body, we all do! **1 Co 12** *"12For as the body is one and has many members, but all the members of that one body, being many, are one body, so also is Christ. 13For by one Spirit we were all baptized into one body – whether Jews or Greeks, whether slaves or free – and have all been made to drink into one Spirit. 14For in fact the body is not one member but many."* Now skip to verse **34**. The inference here is that the failure of a few, on this occasion, would result in judgement on all. Now go back to verse **30**. Who there are "the many" who are weak and sick and dead?

The answer is not necessarily those who had a wrong attitude toward the Lord's supper. Does this mean "Guilt by association"? Well, consider this. If you have a family of four children and one of your sons misbehaves, the people your son has offended will come after the family as a whole and their retribution may fall on one of the other members rather than the one who caused the problem in the first place. Remember Jesus made us interdependent. Also, it is a fact of life that the many innocents suffer because of the wrongful acts of the guilty few.

The failure of the few to discern the Lord's body, or the inability to recognise that the fate of their brethren lay in their hands, meant that when Satan came to oppress some of the members with sickness and disease the unity of the fellowship (necessary for effective intervention for the afflicted members) was not there and the result was "weakness and sickness unto death"

Our welfare lies in each other's hands. No individual, church group or denomination can expect to grow to the fulness of Christ on their own. The entire church is one and, like it or not, we are fully dependent on one another.

Personal Notes

When the people of the world see the church, they need to see unity, love, peace, joy in order to be filled with a desire to be part of it. Instead they see factions, in-fighting, put-downs – you name it – and so the world stays away.

As a journey begins with one step, so the attitude of a small or large group begins with one good example. Make notes of what the Holy Spirit is telling you to do to be such an example and commit yourself to be a light for Christ in this crucial area.

Jas 5 *"⁹Do not grumble against one another, brethren, lest you be condemned. Behold, the Judge is standing at the door! ¹³Is anyone among you suffering? Let him pray. Is anyone cheerful? Let him sing psalms. ¹⁴Is anyone among you sick? Let him call for the elders of the church, and let them pray over him, anointing him with oil in the name of the Lord. ¹⁵And the prayer of faith will save the sick, and the Lord will raise him up. And if he has committed sins, he will be forgiven. ¹⁶Confess your trespasses to one another, and pray for one another, that you may be healed. The effective, fervent prayer of a righteous man avails much. ¹⁹Brethren, if anyone among you wanders from the truth, and someone turns him back, ²⁰let him know that he who turns a sinner from the error of his way will save a soul from death and cover a multitude of sins."*

If, as an individual, you can grasp that and live a life of a good example among your local congregation and refuse to listen to gossip or negative put-downs about other parts of the body of Christ, you will not then have to suffer the condemnation they are currently under. Instead, you can pray for them and exhort them to change and hold out a personal hand of friendship to all those who bear the name of Christ whichever denomination they come from.

Find out the needs of other churches in your area and pray for their members. Don't let any criticism pass your lips concerning the wider church. Be an ambassador for your own church to the wider church in your area. Be generous with what God has given you and don't be put off if your overtures are rebuffed. You will reap a reward for your efforts if you persevere. Some in your own group may resent your efforts to reach out to "those heathen". Just quietly explain why you are doing this and encourage them to join you. You won't change attitudes overnight but never underestimate the power of a good example.

One final point. In the book of Revelation we are told that Christ will marry his Bride (the Church) on his return. **Rev 21** *"⁹Then one of the seven angels who had the seven bowls filled with the seven last plagues came to me and talked with me, saying, 'Come, I will show you the bride, the Lamb's wife.' ¹⁰And he carried me away in the Spirit to a great and high*

Personal Notes

When the people of the world see the church, they need to see unity, love, peace, joy in order to be filled with a desire to be part of it. Instead they see factions, in-fighting, put-downs – you name it – and so the world stays away.

As a journey begins with one step, so the attitude of a small or large group begins with one good example. Make notes of what the Holy Spirit is telling you to do to be such an example and commit yourself to be a light for Christ in this crucial area.

mountain, and showed me the great city, the holy Jerusalem, descending out of heaven from God, *11having the glory of God. Her light was like a most precious stone, like a jasper stone, clear as crystal.*" Can you imagine a more grotesque scene than one where our heavenly Father presents the Bride to Jesus Christ in pieces? Pushing a wheel barrow down the aisle with disjointed body parts dumped on top of one another? That will never be allowed to happen. The church has been warned that judgement begins at the household of God and we are presently under that judgement. The consequences of unfaithfulness are already being felt and our repentance and renewal to our first love are an absolute top priority.

Rev 3 "*14And to the angel of the church of the Laodiceans write, 'These things says the Amen, the Faithful and True Witness, the Beginning of the creation of God: 15I know your works, that you are neither cold nor hot. I could wish you were cold or hot. 16So then, because you are lukewarm, and neither cold nor hot, I will vomit you out of My mouth.' 17Because you say, 'I am rich, have become wealthy, and have need of nothing' – and do not know that you are wretched, miserable, poor, blind, and naked – 18I counsel you to buy from Me gold refined in the fire, that you may be rich; and white garments, that you may be clothed, that the shame of your nakedness may not be revealed; and anoint your eyes with eye salve, that you may see. 19As many as I love, I rebuke and chasten. Therefore be zealous and repent.*"

CHAPTER FIVE

Medical Intervention – Does God Approve?

Most, if not many, working within the medical community have compassion, empathy, love, commitment, even self-sacrifice inherent within them when caring for their patients. But they are not gifted to heal with faith. By contrast, Christ had all of the above but he never bandaged a wound nor handed out pills. He healed and intervened by faith. It is faith that moves God. The Kingdom of God responds to faith! If you have the faith to heal a spot, then precisely that same power can raise the dead!

There are many denominations within the body of Christ that wrestle with this question. Is it a lack of faith for someone to seek medical help to ease a distressing physical or mental condition? The short answer is no! However, all Christians are told to live by faith. We are advised to turn to God with all our problems, no matter how small or big they may be. **Lk 11** *"⁵And He said to them, 'Which of you shall have a friend, and go to him at midnight' and say to him, 'Friend, lend me three loaves; ⁶for a friend of mine has come to me on his journey, and I have nothing to set before him'; ⁷and he will answer from within and say, 'Do not trouble me; the door is now shut, and my children are with me in bed; I cannot rise and give to you?' ⁸I say to you, though he will not rise and give to him because he is his friend, yet because of his persistence he will rise and give him as many as he needs. '⁹So I say to you, ask, and it will be given to you; seek, and you will find; knock, and it will be opened to you. ¹⁰For everyone who asks receives, and he who seeks finds, and to him who knocks it will be opened. ¹¹If a son asks for bread from any father among you, will he give*

him a stone? Or if he asks for a fish, will he give him a serpent instead of a
fish? ¹²Or if he asks for an egg, will he offer him a scorpion? ¹³If you then,
being evil, know how to give good gifts to your children, how much more will
your heavenly Father give the Holy Spirit to those who ask Him'!"

The Bible also reveals that there is a process we need to go through to receive the divine intervention we are seeking. But there are some who, either through lack of knowledge, poor counsel or just plain fear, appear unwilling to go through this process and prefer to rely purely on worldly means to ease that condition.

Suppose a Christian man wakes up one morning with pains in his chest. It's not that bad but he thinks it would be wise to go and get himself checked out at the local hospital. So far, there is nothing wrong with what he is doing, though he should pray and ask that the doctor will make an accurate diagnosis of his condition.

After going through several tests, he meets with the consultant who gravely informs him that he has a terminal heart condition that will require major surgery. The prognosis is not good; the patient will be on powerful drugs for the rest of his life which the consultant esti-mates will be around two to three years if the surgery is successful.

The immediate response of anyone receiving this news is shock. Nothing shakes us up more than to be confronted by our own mor-tality. Our patient tells his family the bad news and a grim foreboding appears to settle over the house. Future plans and dreams are shelved. What seemed to be so important now appears trite and irrelevant.

But a decision is yet to be made. Should he proceed with surgery, and all the consequences that can flow from that, or should he take his chances and wait for a miracle?

The Scriptural response is crystal clear to anyone facing such a dilemma. "Let everyone receive according to their faith." **Mt 21** *"²¹So Jesus answered and said to them, 'Assuredly, I say to you, if you have*

Personal Notes

As you increase in understanding, your faith (belief) should also increase. This will increase your wisdom and give prudence to your decision-making. Now, as you pray, your prayers will exhibit your understanding of the will of the Father. And if you know the will of the Father and ask according to that, then you know for a fact that you will receive what you are asking for.

Continue your witness statement and make the kind of notes that you can refer back to later. Give thanks as your deliverance draws near.

faith and do not doubt, you will not only do what was done to the fig tree, *but also if you say to this mountain, Be removed and be cast into the sea,' it* *will be done.* ^{22}*And whatever things you ask in prayer, believing, you will* *receive."* **Jn 3** *"*^{27}*John answered and said, 'A man can receive nothing* *unless it has been given to him from heaven'."* If you are absolutely convinced that God wants you to proceed with the surgery and you're trusting Him with the outcome then go ahead and do that. However, if you are convinced that surgery is not the way to go and you are convinced that God has both the power to heal you, and that He desires to heal you, then beware for you will have to go through an accountability test which is primarily what this book is about. An Old Testament example of accountability can be found in **2 Kings 5:1–14** in which a powerful man could only receive a major healing once he had humbled himself in the sight of both God and man, which for him was very humiliating.

Some Christian leaders teach that the only things you have to do to receive miraculous healing are to deny the power of sickness over your life, to actively proclaim that you are healed by the stripes of Jesus, to trust completely in his deliverance – never doubting, to believe that you will receive, and to wait patiently. All these things are true, but there is a lot more to it than just that. A Christian could do all these things, without being healed, right up to the day of their death. I know. I've attended their funerals.

I confess to being a little irritated sometimes when I hear some Christian leaders who keep teaching these five points and highlighting the successes – which make-up a tiny proportion of those that are faithfully following these points.

Those for whom the five points do not appear to be working could be forgiven for thinking that God has abandoned them when, having done everything their leaders have taught them, find absolutely nothing has changed. It is at this point that many Christians will forget about the miraculous part and start concentrating on the secular options. More pills, more potions, more operations, more chemo and

Personal Notes

As you increase in understanding, your faith (belief) should also increase. This will increase your wisdom and give prudence to your decision-making. Now, as you pray, your prayers will exhibit your understanding of the will of the Father. And if you know the will of the Father and ask according to that, then you know for a fact that you will receive what you are asking for.

Continue your witness statement and make the kind of notes that you can refer back to later. Give thanks as your deliverance draws near.

maybe just a nod towards God that He will assist the process. Beyond that – and I know this is brutal – *they won't trust him!*

So what about the family who chooses to go with the major operation and trust God with the outcome? Well, I could sugar-coat the answer but it wouldn't help. The process, described in this book and that includes all the scriptures dealing with this subject, cannot be bypassed. The operation may be a success. The patient may get some short-term relief. But the spiritual condition that prompted this test in the first place is still there and it will just be a matter of time before something else happens. **Heb12** *"5And you have forgotten the exhortation which speaks to you as to sons: 'My son, do not despise the chastening of the Lord, Nor be discouraged when you are rebuked by Him; 6For whom the Lord loves He chastens, And scourges every son whom He receives.' 7If you endure chastening, God deals with you as with sons; for what son is there whom a father does not chasten? 8But if you are without chastening, of which all have become partakers, then you are illegitimate and not sons. 9Furthermore, we have had human fathers who corrected us, and we paid them respect. Shall we not much more readily be in subjection to the Father of spirits and live? 10For they indeed for a few days chastened us as seemed best to them, but He for our profit, that we may be partakers of His holiness. 11Now no chastening seems to be joyful for the present, but painful; nevertheless, afterward it yields the peaceable fruit of righteousness to those who have been trained by it. 12Therefore strengthen the hands which hang down, and the feeble knees, 13and make straight paths for your feet, so that what is lame may not be dislocated, but rather be healed."*

It's true, God is very merciful and patient with us, but when something has to be sorted out, your eternal future comes first. Remember, you were bought with a great price! Giving over your life to Christ is your *reasonable* service. You agreed to all the conditions of the new covenant, to be transformed by the renewing of your mind, to be a witness to this world, both by example and by sharing the gospel. You were told that you would have to work out your salvation with trembling and fear.

Personal Notes

As you increase in understanding, your faith (belief) should also increase. This will increase your wisdom and give prudence to your decision-making. Now, as you pray, your prayers will exhibit your understanding of the will of the Father. And if you know the will of the Father and ask according to that, then you know for a fact that you will receive what you are asking for.

Continue your witness statement and make the kind of notes that you can refer back to later. Give thanks as your deliverance draws near.

God faithfully chastises all those who belong to Him, as a faithful dad does to his son. This may not be a popular message but it is the truth and only the truth will set you free from your present predicament.

Medical intervention is fine within the corrective process, if that is what God is leading you to do, but that process cannot and will not be avoided! Read **Amos 4:6–12**. The corrective process exists throughout the Bible and just dealing with the symptoms is rarely the answer.

God is no respecter of persons. That's true but He deals with us on an individual basis and our personal growth rate is determined by the unique strengths and weaknesses present within us and grow we must! What was acceptable and winked at last year may be unacceptable this year. How many parents would accept the behaviour of a five-year-old in their teenager? **Jn 15** *"¹I am the true vine, and My Father is the vinedresser. ²Every branch in Me that does not bear fruit He takes away; and every branch that bears fruit He prunes, that it may bear more fruit. ³You are already clean because of the word which I have spoken to you. ⁴Abide in Me, and I in you. As the branch cannot bear fruit of itself, unless it abides in the vine, neither can you, unless you abide in Me. ⁵I am the vine, you are the branches. He who abides in Me, and I in him, bears much fruit; for without Me you can do nothing. ⁶If anyone does not abide in Me, he is cast out as a branch and is withered; and they gather them and throw them into the fire, and they are burned. ⁷If you abide in Me, and My words abide in you, you will ask what you desire, and it shall be done for you. ⁸By this My Father is glorified, that you bear much fruit; so you will be My disciples."*

The Holy Spirit speaks to us in a still small voice. We're not likely to hear God if we are preoccupied with personal gratification, or we have allowed our personal relationship with Him to grow stale, or we're distracted by personal worries that should have been handed over to Him. Or maybe we did hear but chose to ignore it because it would upset our comfortable routine or we feared the unseen if we obeyed and did what was being asked of us.

Personal Notes

As you increase in understanding, your faith (belief) should also increase. This will increase your wisdom and give prudence to your decision-making. Now, as you pray, your prayers will exhibit your understanding of the will of the Father. And if you know the will of the Father and ask according to that, then you know for a fact that you will receive what you are asking for.

Continue your witness statement and make the kind of notes that you can refer back to later. Give thanks as your deliverance draws near.

So, whether by choice or distraction, it is possible for us not to hear when God tells us to change or do something. Consequently, God moves on and we are stuck where we were.

I want to pause and expand on this point for a moment. Please understand, you may not have done anything wrong in the context of deliberate sin but you may have been called to change a significant part of your life in order to fall into God's personal plan for you. Let me give you an example from my own life. I have been a Christian for eighteen years. Two years ago, I felt prompted to do more and more writing. But this prompting came at a time when, after years of struggling, my construction business had really begun to take-off. I had earned a good reputation and business was flooding in. Debts were being cleared and I had an opportunity to become financially independent, maybe get married, go on holiday . . . Life was looking good!

I answered the call to write but there was just no time to get it done and run the business. Something had to give. Fortunately, my relationship with God was pretty solid and when I prayed about this situation, He made it clear to me what should come first.

Mt 6 "²⁴*No one can serve two masters; for either he will hate the one and love the other, or else he will be loyal to the one and despise the other. You cannot serve God and mammon.* ²⁵*Therefore I say to you, do not worry about your life, what you will eat or what you will drink; nor about your body, what you will put on. Is not life more than food and the body more than clothing?* ²⁶*Look at the birds of the air, for they neither sow nor reap nor gather into barns; yet your heavenly Father feeds them. Are you not of more value than they?* ²⁷*Which of you by worrying can add one cubit to his stature?* ²⁸*So why do you worry about clothing? Consider the lilies of the field, how they grow: they neither toil nor spin;* ²⁹*and yet I say to you that even Solomon in all his glory was not arrayed like one of these.* ³⁰*Now if God so clothes the grass of the field, which today is, and tomorrow is thrown into the oven, will He not much more clothe you, O you of little faith?'* ³¹*Therefore do not worry, saying, 'What shall we eat?' or 'What shall we drink?' or 'What shall we wear?'* ³²*For after all these things the Gentiles seek. For your heavenly Father knows*

Personal Notes

As you increase in understanding, your faith (belief) should also increase. This will increase your wisdom and give prudence to your decision-making. Now, as you pray, your prayers will exhibit your understanding of the will of the Father. And if you know the will of the Father and ask according to that, then you know for a fact that you will receive what you are asking for.

Continue your witness statement and make the kind of notes that you can refer back to later. Give thanks as your deliverance draws near.

that you need all these things. ³³But seek first the kingdom of God and His righteousness, and all these things shall be added to you."

The very next day I began to wind the business down so that I worked one day a week. My income became less than a third of what it was, yet my outgoings stayed pretty much the same. Was I concerned? Well maybe a little nervous but I have no doubt that I did the right thing. But what do you suppose would have happened had I chosen to ignore God?

If we don't listen, God moves on and everything goes with Him including our hedge of protection. All of a sudden we are vulnerable! The warning signs are there but we're too wrapped up in our personal lives to pay them any heed and before we know it, we're facing a personal catastrophe.

Because we're discussing medical intervention, we can use the medical process of diagnosis and treatment recommendations as an analogy for God's corrective process:

First, acknowledge something is wrong. Something in your spiritual life and your relationship with God is not functioning properly. Now, go before the Great Physician; seek His counsel; repent of all your known faults and pray for the strength to change. Draw near to God and He will draw near to you!

Go see your Priest/Elder/Minister. Ask God to show them where your faults lie and have the courage to accept their critique. Now, examine your relationships. First, with your spouse, then your children, then your extended family. Remember this is the diagnosis period where you are trying to find out what you may have been doing wrong. Next, examine your relationship with your church family (*see* chapter 4), then your neighbours and co-workers. Be open to correction. Take every issue that arises and humble yourself before almighty God, seeking His forgiveness wherever you find you have been in error. Study the new covenant and respond to each issue that arises according to the commands of your Saviour.

Personal Notes

As you increase in understanding, your faith (belief) should also increase. This will increase your wisdom and give prudence to your decision-making. Now, as you pray, your prayers will exhibit your understanding of the will of the Father. And if you know the will of the Father and ask according to that, then you know for a fact that you will receive what you are asking for.

Continue your witness statement and make the kind of notes that you can refer back to later. Give thanks as your deliverance draws near.

What you're now going through is the treatment phase. You may feel embarrassed, even humiliated. That's good! If it's hurting, it's working! This is just the beginning. As you follow through this book and you are faithful and refuse to quit, God will lead you towards the final answer and your healing will quickly follow. **Isa 66** *"²On this one will I look: he who is poor and of a contrite spirit and who trembles at My word."* **Isa 58** *"⁹Then you shall call, and the Lord will answer; You shall cry, and He will say, 'Here I am.' 'If you take away the yoke from your midst, The pointing of the finger, and speaking wickedness, ¹⁰If you extend your soul to the hungry And satisfy the afflicted soul, Then your light shall dawn in the darkness, And your darkness shall be as the noonday. ¹¹The Lord will guide you continually, And satisfy your soul in drought, And strengthen your bones; You shall be like a watered garden, And like a spring of water, whose waters do not fail'."*

Do not be surprised if the final answer comes from a source you would not have thought to check. You may have to go outside your denomination to find the answers that you seek, or your "enemy" may have the answer for you, if you're humble enough to listen.

If the medical community are aware of your condition and you have chosen not to follow all their recommendations and they question you on this, be honest! Openly and boldly proclaim that you are seeking the help of Jesus Christ with this problem that, as a Christian, you are confident in God's promise to heal. **Mt 10** *"³²If you will confess my Name before men, I will confess your name before my Father!"*

Now, as the following matter has sometimes come up in the courts, I feel I should address this in this book: If you have a sick child and you are unsure whether or not to pursue medical treatment to correct her condition, don't be! You have a responsibility for her welfare that is overseen by a secular authority. No authority exists without God and to wilfully withhold recommended medical treatment from a child who, by virtue of age, cannot assent to treatment without parental approval is to disobey that authority and consequently bring the church into disrepute.

Personal Notes

As you increase in understanding, your faith (belief) should also increase. This will increase your wisdom and give prudence to your decision-making. Now, as you pray, your prayers will exhibit your understanding of the will of the Father. And if you know the will of the Father and ask according to that, then you know for a fact that you will receive what you are asking for.

Continue your witness statement and make the kind of notes that you can refer back to later. Give thanks as your deliverance draws near.

There is no Biblical sanction for that kind of behaviour. Of course you will pray. Of course you can get a second opinion. Of course you must examine yourself to determine why your child fell sick in the first place (*see* chapter 1). But those authorities exist to safeguard the welfare of all children and your patient, kind, thankful co-operation with them is a Biblical requirement.

Finally, how should we treat emergency cases? A sudden stroke, a car crash, an explosion. The urgency of the need does not preclude Godly intervention, sometimes a three-word prayer can do wonders. "Father, help me!" can yield amazing results.

A few years ago, I was driving home late at night when I was subjected to a full frontal 140 miles-per-hour impact from a bigger, heavier car being driven by a drunk driver. My car was virtually demolished and all emergency personnel were astonished that I was not dead nor, at least,severely disabled. I did have some injuries but given the severity of the crash, my survival was an amazing miracle. Now, I personally do not like hospitals; but I was not in any fit state to argue with the paramedics, so I offered up a silent prayer that they wouldn't have to operate and that my face would not be hideously scarred for life.

At that hospital I was treated like a king. A reconstructive surgeon rebuilt my nose and mouth and amazingly I suffered no broken bones or internal organ damage. There was massive bruising and I could hardly move. I was taken home twenty-four hours later and one week later I was back at church, almost completely healed.

Yes, God uses the medical community sometimes for our benefit but He knows how to look after His own with or without their help. Our responsibility is to remain faithful to Him at all times, obey Him, trust Him, follow Him wherever He leads us. If we do that, we need never fear in the day of adversity.

Finally, this chapter would be incomplete without acknowledging the subject of appropriate diet and exercise. There are numerous

Personal Notes

As you increase in understanding, your faith (belief) should also increase. This will increase your wisdom and give prudence to your decision-making. Now, as you pray, your prayers will exhibit your understanding of the will of the Father. And if you know the will of the Father and ask according to that, then you know for a fact that you will receive what you are asking for.

Continue your witness statement and make the kind of notes that you can refer back to later. Give thanks as your deliverance draws near.

books available to Christians and unbelievers alike, where the effects of poor diet and lack of exercise have been attributed to ill-health.

Obviously, we should take care of ourselves and our family. We should ensure balanced nutrition, a proper exercise regimen and avoid taking anything to excess. This includes drinking alcohol, eating fatty and sugary foods, smoking, taking drugs and any sedentary pursuits.

But remember, our human condition is often a very good indicator of our spiritual condition and if we find ourselves bound to addictions or prone to any excess in any area of life, we should recognise our need to seek our Creator's help to bring balance back into our lives.

2 Ti 1 *"7For God has not given us a spirit of fear, but of power and of love and of a sound mind."*

CHAPTER SIX

Who Are Your Ninevites?

This is a crucial insight for all Christian men and women. This book has been written to accomplish a dual purpose: To help you out of your present crisis and to prepare those members who have been called to heal (*see* chapter 2).

Before we begin, you will need to carefully read the book of **Jonah** and understand the story flow.

God tells Jonah to go to Nineveh and call upon them to repent of their wicked ways or God will bring devastation upon them. Jonah's immediate response is to try and get as far away from God as he can. Why?

As the story proceeds we discover that Jonah has a deep-seated hatred for the Ninevites and we can only surmise the reason why. My guess is that at some point in the past some Ninevites had caused great harm either to Jonah himself or to people that he cared about. God did not expand on the "wickedness" He spoke about. The last thing that Jonah wanted to do was to be used by God to preach a message of repentance and for the people to then respond to that message and escape the punishment that Jonah felt they richly deserved.

So he ran away. If you review the previous chapter, you can see what happens when we refuse to obey God concerning the work He has for us to do. In Jonah's case, it cost him his life.

It must have been apparent to God how much Jonah hated the Ninevites and I'm sure Jonah was not the only man of God that He could have used to send that message, so why did God choose Jonah?

He chose Jonah *because* he hated the Ninevites! There was a major flaw in Jonah's character that had to be corrected. Jonah viewed these people as not being worthy of God's mercy. In his mind he judged them. The motivating spirit behind such a response is pride. By judging them, he elevated himself as being more righteous than them. He failed to understand that the only reason why he was not practising the same wickedness as them was because he was already a recipient of God's mercy.

Let's move this story to a more modern setting. Of all the people on the earth, who do you despise the most? Is it based on nationality, race, religion, politics or culture? Or is it based on social and/or criminal behaviour, such as murderers, rapists, child abusers, wife beaters, abortionists, homosexuals, couples who divorce, liars, thieves, vandals, drunkards, drug-pushers, pimps, prostitutes, dictators?

Once again, I'll use myself as an example: When I was growing up I encountered bullying, both verbal and physical, on a daily basis from the day I started school at the age of five, to the day I left at the age of sixteen. I was fearful and filled with hatred towards anyone who used their superior strength, talent or intellect to dominate, control or bully anyone weaker than themselves. Men who beat their wives, rapists, men of violence in any capacity were worthy only of death. My desire was that whatever pain they had inflicted should be visited upon them a thousand-fold. Then, maybe they would be able to empathise with the terrible suffering they had caused. This attitude definitely affected my relationship with God. My capacity for mercy was extremely limited. It was very easy to have compassion upon the vic-

Personal Notes

At this stage of the book, we are beginning to overlap the subject of your personal deliverance onto the subject of your future commission.

Your commission will be something that you must pursue of your own volition. You will find yourself empathising with a particular group of people in a particular kind of situation. Our Father will clarify the part He wants you to play as we proceed.

Be alert and attentive to what the Holy Spirit is telling you about your future. Note down what occurs to you. Keep looking-up the scriptures in your own Bible, and keep praying for wisdom.

tims. I would never tire of helping them, look after them and be patient with them, but the bullies? Forget it!

So what did God do? Through my business, personal relationships, church life and almost every encounter, He brought me into contact with people who had behaved in this way. To say that I resented this would be an understatement. My cry to God was, "Look Father, you don't understand, I became a Christian in large part so that I could be a blessing to the victims of this world. Send me to a rape crisis counselling centre, let me work with battered wives and fatherless children, use me to help *them*!"

His reply, "That's exactly what I am doing!"

Does that answer make sense to you? It has taken me almost to the present day to fully comprehend what God was saying.

In summary, the answer is this: my human nature is exactly the same as the person who is the most violent, sadistic, evil person you have ever heard of. Given enough time and the right set of circumstances, I could become just as bad, if not worse, than that same person. The only reason I have not descended that far is because of divine inter-vention and mercy in my life. When Christ was flogged and crucified, he knew that the people who did this; from Judas to the high priests, to the Roman soldiers, would not have had any desire to do this if they had had the Holy Spirit and a personal relationship with God. That is why he said, "Father forgive them because they don't know what they're doing!"

This understanding brings with it a whole new set of responsibilities, particularly where the Church is concerned. Some parts of the Church have got themselves into trouble where they feel compelled to indulge in something called "sin discrimination"! This is where some sins are highlighted as being especially evil and those that practise them are more certain to be condemned than everybody else, such as homosexuality and abortion. A direct consequence of this has been to alienate large sections of the community and foster

Personal Notes

At this stage of the book, we are beginning to overlap the subject of your personal deliverance onto the subject of your future commission.

Your commission will be something that you must pursue of your own volition. You will find yourself empathising with a particular group of people in a particular kind of situation. Our Father will clarify the part He wants you to play as we proceed.

Be alert and attentive to what the Holy Spirit is telling you about your future. Note down what occurs to you. Keep looking-up the scriptures in your own Bible, and keep praying for wisdom.

widespread resentment against the Church as a whole. We are viewed as being self-righteous and divisive and this hurts our effectiveness in fulfilling the great commission. Jesus Christ is the final authority on questions such as this and he speaks of universal condemnation on all who sin and fall short of the glory of God. (Look again at chapter 1)

As Christians, we cannot pick and choose what we like from the scriptures. If we accept one part, we accept it all.

So back to the question, "Who are your Ninevites?", who is least deserving of mercy in your opinion? I can tell you with absolute conviction that there is a Jonah in each one of us and if you cannot answer the above question because you're not sure, or you think it doesn't apply to you, then you need to go before God and ask Him to show you. There were times when King David would go before God and ask Him to search his heart and cleanse him from all unrighteousness, **Ps 139** *"23Search me, O God, and know my heart; Try me, and know my anxieties; 24And see if there is any wicked way in me, And lead me in the way everlasting."* That is a good example for all of us to follow.

When Jesus said pray for your enemies, bless those who curse you and forgive those who despitefully use you (**Matthew 5:44**). He was not offering advice. These were specific commands for all Christians. We have been told to be doers of the Word and not just hearers only, deceiving ourselves (**James 1:22**). Our obedience in these areas places these troubled people in God's hands and brings His intervention into their lives. You help to restrain evil through your obedience. For instance: a bully will be less inclined to continue on his destructive way. Our prayers and intercessions for victims will be answered when we submit ourselves to God's perfect ways and stop judging situations according to our own so-called wisdom which is inherently flawed.

A direct consequence of obedience is an increase in faith which can, and will, move mountains. Perfect obedience to Christ's commands

Personal Notes

At this stage of the book, we are beginning to overlap the subject of your personal deliverance onto the subject of your future commission.

Your commission will be something that you must pursue of your own volition. You will find yourself empathising with a particular group of people in a particular kind of situation. Our Father will clarify the part He wants you to play as we proceed.

Be alert and attentive to what the Holy Spirit is telling you about your future. Note down what occurs to you. Keep looking-up the scriptures in your own Bible, and keep praying for wisdom.

is impossible without submitting ourselves under the power of the Holy Spirit who will give us both the will and the means to obey.

We must learn to trust our heavenly Father in the same way Jesus did. In **Matthew 18:3**, Jesus said, *"Except you become as little children, you will not enter the kingdom of God* (and all the power contained therein).*"* A little child trusts his father and believes everything that he is told by his father. That level of humility, submission, obedience and faith will take the church into the realm of the miraculous, which is what we need if we are to complete the divine commission that has been entrusted to us.

Remember, you are part of that. Don't let your Ninevites stand in the way!

CHAPTER SEVEN

You Are Not *Job*

Yes, it is a strange title. But it refers to the book of Job in the Old Testament that tells a story of a righteous man who was put through the most bitter of trials.

We are going to examine why this happened, what was its purpose and why many church teachers have been inaccurate in their interpretation of the outcome of this story.

First, as with the previous chapter, I ask that you read the book of Job and take notes as to what parts of the story stand out for you and what questions it raises.

The story of Job is a source of mystery and wonder to those who have read it. Here we have a righteous man with a deep and abiding respect for God, who is suddenly hit with a major calamity with God's full permission. In one day, he loses all his children, nearly all his employees are murdered and a hugely successful business is bankrupted overnight. If that isn't enough, he wakes one morning to find himself covered with boils from head to foot. If you have ever suffered from just one boil, you will have some idea of what a horrendous affliction this was.

Don't forget that Job was married. Can you possibly imagine how Job's wife must have felt? No wonder she said, "Oh just curse God and die!" They were both in a state of extreme shock. Where did all this come from? What had they done that could possibly have merited this? No wonder, when Job's friends showed up to comfort him, the only possible conclusion they could come to was that Job had committed some grievous sin.

I have heard and read strange and damning interpretations of the reasons behind why God allowed this tragedy to befall Job. I have heard people use this to justify ill health, afflictions and tragedies in other people's lives. Many students of the Word of God have tried to figure out what on earth it was that Job did wrong or what other possible reason could there be for God to test Job in such a destructive way.

First, what did Job do wrong? Answer: Nothing! Right at the beginning of the story, we are told that Job was a righteous man and blameless before God. In numerous books throughout the Old Testament, God tells His people that He will bless those who walk uprightly and provide protection, prosperity, good health, good relationships, peace, you name it, to those who honour His ways. God is a rewarder of those who seek Him, who tremble at His word and are careful to obey all of His commandments. Job was such a man!

So if this wasn't punishment for sin or disobedience, then what was it?

Well, we know that Abraham was also such a man. In **Genesis 22** we know that he was tested in a major way when he was told by God to sacrifice his one and only son Isaac. Why? So that God would know beyond a shadow of a doubt that Abraham trusted Him above everything.

Oh, okay, so this was a test to determine if Job would trust God and be faithful even when things got tough. There is just one problem with that conclusion. In Abraham's case, he was given something specific to do. His obedience proved his faithfulness. In Job's case he wasn't given anything to do. There was absolute silence from God. Job had a grieving, inconsolable wife, a horrible skin condition from which there was no relief and friends who could only offer accusations rather than support. He had lost all his children, all visible means of support and

Personal Notes

Countless thousands in the Christian faith have denied themselves the faith to be healed because of wrong assumptions made about the experiences of Job. This explanation sets the record straight and will prove to be a great blessing to all who advise afflicted Christians.

Make your own notes about what stands out for you from this teaching and share your findings whenever you get the opportunity.

could see no end in sight for all this distress. People have committed suicide over much less. In fact, Job contemplates death many times and who could blame him.

Toward the end of the story, when God does come to intervene, He never says that this trial was brought to test Job's faithfulness as He did with Abraham. In fact, the discourse between the Lord and Job is a very disconcerting one. He makes absolutely clear His dominion and pre-eminence over all His creation, that He will do what He has chosen to do and no one can withstand Him.

We sometimes forget the awesome power and majesty of our Creator, and that can really hinder our personal relationship with Him and our effectiveness as a church. He doesn't exist for us; we exist for Him and that was the message the Lord conveyed to Job.

So, why did this happen? God gave us this account for a reason. He expects us to learn from Job's experience so we need to find the intent behind the story. At the beginning, when Satan reports back to God on what he's been up to, it is God who points out Job to Satan and effectively challenges Satan regarding this righteous and obedient servant.

We also learn that Job was incredibly prosperous, that he held a very high and influential position in his country. Everybody either knew him or knew about him. A modern equivalent might be Bill Gates of Microsoft, very wealthy and very well-known. If something happened to him or his family the whole of America would know. Therefore, it is a pretty safe assumption that when tragedy befell Job, everyone would hear about it.

God had made sure that Job would rise high in the position he held in his Country. His position, family, possessions and abundant blessings were not just for his personal enjoyment, but so that God could use him as an example of how God blesses the upright.

Personal Notes

Countless thousands in the Christian faith have denied themselves the faith to be healed because of wrong assumptions made about the experiences of Job. This explanation sets the record straight and will prove to be a great blessing to all who advise afflicted Christians.

Make your own notes about what stands out for you from this teaching and share your findings whenever you get the opportunity.

Job was generous with what he had been given. He had wisdom and favour in the eyes of men: Job represented the gospel in his day!

This trial was not primarily for Job's personal benefit. It is important to note that at the time this all happened Job did not have a commission from the Lord to preach the gospel in a hostile world as we do today. Our faithfulness in carrying out that work can and may lead to violence, oppression, even death. The Lord never exercised any such claim on Job's life or anyone else on earth at that time. But at a pre-ordained time, the Lord chose to use everything He had given to Job to send a message to the people in Job's country. They were astonished at what had happened to this man of faith and their response would undoubtedly be: that they feared (greatly respected) the Lord God of Job. His life was God's witness to that generation.

This is why it is so unwise to use what happened to Job as some kind of explanation for something that is going wrong in your life. You are not Job and neither am I. We have a very specific job to do, very specific commands to follow and, if we are totally faithful in carrying that out, we will encounter opposition as a direct consequence of obeying God. **Mk 13** *"⁹But watch out for yourselves, for they will deliver you up to councils, and you will be beaten in the synagogues. You will be brought before rulers and kings for My sake, for a testimony to them."*

Illness, injury, mental problems are all connected to our being out of step with where we should be at this time. Healing will come as soon as we re-align ourselves with God. I hesitate to write this next part; but I cannot conceive of a single instance where these problems are deliberately brought onto us by God to help us spread the gospel and I know of no set of scriptures that attest to that. Poverty and illness are not a witness.

Jesus Christ healed. He blessed. He produced abundance. There is no record of the disciples getting sick around Christ. The early church blossomed and grew exponentially because of their love and generosity to one another as they faithfully obeyed the commands of Jesus Christ. When some of the world's attitudes started to find their

Personal Notes

Countless thousands in the Christian faith have denied themselves the faith to be healed because of wrong assumptions made about the experiences of Job. This explanation sets the record straight and will prove to be a great blessing to all who advise afflicted Christians.

Make your own notes about what stands out for you from this teaching and share your findings whenever you get the opportunity.

way into the church, they brought sickness and disease, and divine intervention waned in direct proportion to the reduction in obedience and faith.

This book is about reclaiming that first love, and it begins with you. Don't let anyone try and tell you that your trial is a Job-like experience and that you'll have to wait and do nothing until God intervenes. Let the scriptures guide you into all truth. So be wary of "wolves in sheep's clothing". Jesus said you will know them by their fruits (**Matthew 7:20**). Be wary and always ask for discernment.

The following comments have been added to explain what some people feel was a major injustice to Job and his family when they lost their original children.

A secular commentator on the book of Job expressed his outrage at God's "callousness" in wiping out Job's family; that his original seven sons and three daughters were lost to him forever; that no amount of subsequent blessings could make up for such a tragic loss; that surely Job and his wife would be mourning the loss of their children for the rest of their lives. This is not an invalid point to make and, as children of the light, we are responsible for the defence of the gospel. First, we have to remember that our Father is motivated by love. God is a giver, He withholds nothing that is good for us. Through Christ we receive undeserved pardon for our sins and access to eternal life. Everything that He asks of us is ultimately for our own benefit.

Second, you should be aware that there are many prophecies that indicate that all the unsaved (including Job's children) will be resurrected back to physical life at a future point in time. No-one is "lost"! However, there is dogmatic doctrine that insistently teaches otherwise, but such a doctrine cannot withstand the forensic scrutiny of scripture. This subject will be tackled in greater depth in the very near future and will frankly electrify many parts of the church with its conclusions and all from the Word of God!

Personal Notes

Countless thousands in the Christian faith have denied themselves the faith to be healed because of wrong assumptions made about the experiences of Job. This explanation sets the record straight and will prove to be a great blessing to all who advise afflicted Christians.

Make your own notes about what stands out for you from this teaching and share your findings whenever you get the opportunity.

This may come as a shock, but when you examine the original context of Christ's teachings on the subject of "hellfire" (or eternal death) the warning is not directed at unbelievers. It is a cautionary indictment against born-again, spirit-filled believers who, having tasted, comprehended, understood and participated in the grace of Jesus Christ, turn against that faith and choose consciously to go back to their former life, thereby bringing shame and condemnation on the Holy Spirit. Now if that condition remains, and that person stays unrepentant then, at the conclusion of their physical life, their eternal fate is sealed. There will surely be but a few who would ever choose such a path, but God makes clear that there will be some.

Judgement does indeed begin at the household of God. At this moment the world is not under judgement but we are. Everything we think, say and do is being recorded and evaluated and judgement accorded as per the conditions outlined in the new covenant. If you are afraid that you might be one of those people who is now beyond redemption, fear not! The unrepentant person is unconcerned about his fate and refuses to heed warnings about his spiritual condition.

CHAPTER EIGHT

The Science of Miraculous Healing

This is a world with genetic engineering, plasma energy, micro transmitters, keyhole surgery and embryonic stem cell research, to name but a few. In recent years the sharing of collective wisdom and research exchange has been made possible because of the new universal medium we call the internet.

Approximately ten million scientists, researchers, teachers and professors share and collaborate on breakthroughs, new ideas and inventions on a daily basis across the globe. The explosion of knowledge, just in the last ten years has been astonishing. It seems there is almost nothing that can be imagined that cannot be invented.

No longer do language, culture, even religion, represent the barrier to learning that they have done in the past. The economy is global. The collective institutions of man, if they are to mean anything today, must be global in structure and co-operation.

Older generations can only gape in wonder as they see a lifetime of wisdom and hard-won experience being eclipsed by the latest fad of psychologists, social engineers and behaviour modification programmes. If you don't get with it, you are regarded as a fossilised throw-back to a dim, distant and ignorant past. Where does God exist in all this?

"He doesn't!" cries the sceptic. "He belongs in a museum along with all the other superstitious paraphernalia of a bygone era." There has been a backlash of course. Many traditional religions have resurfaced with a new face that is more in keeping with the shiny new elements of modern-day thinking and living. Re-branded, re-packaged, digitally re-mastered, the old crusty images have received a radical makeover.

There's just one tiny hitch to this brave new world order (Actually there are several). We still get to die. We still possess the same human nature of greed, selfishness and one-up-man-ship that has marked our experience in the past. And we are still one hundred per cent dependent on the natural resources of the earth to breathe, eat, drink and sustain our fleshly existence.

Ecc 1 *"⁹That which has been is what will be, That which is done is what will be done, And there is nothing new under the sun."* So basically, nothing has changed, apart from a few more labour-saving devices, some new methodology in manufacturing, a few medical breakthroughs and an abundance of new ideas, of which most are rooted in foolishness because they're not based on the revelation of God's word to mankind.

And then you read a book like this, in which believers like me insist that miracles can still happen, that divine intervention can become the norm rather than the exception, and that the gospel has more relevance today than it has had throughout the last 2000 years.

The sins of mankind are the same. The consequences are the same. A great deal of time, money and intellect has been expended to alleviate the worst effects of some of these consequences but you cannot subvert the created order of things. Jesus Christ now sits at the right hand of God and all authority over all creation has been given to him (**Matthew 28:18**). He sustains the created order by the Word of his mouth. If you or I need something to change, He is the one we need to go to. Man's own ingenuity can only carry him so far before the laws of accountability catch up to him.

Personal Notes

No doubt, you will have encountered in the media the issue of medical ethics. When confronted with sickness and disease for which there is no known secular cure, some people will go to extraordinary lengths to find a remedy rather than confront the cause.

This has resulted in attempts to clone human beings to enable harvesting of their organs. Spinal injuries, Althzeimer's disease, brainstem disfunction; all will be curable in time say the experts. But, to achieve this, they are forced into extending the bounds of common sense and reason into uncharted territory. The result has been cruel and unusual experimentation on animals and some unwilling humans.

Now do you see why it is so important for the whole church to rediscover and apply the healing promises of God and to share that good news with the whole earth. "Repentance brings healing!"

Could you go to the established medical authorities of your Country with that message without first backing it up with real life examples? What do you think? What part can you play?

Please write down what you and your church could do.

I've included this chapter because the perception of miraculous healing in our sceptical, science-has-all-the-answers, world; is not seen as any kind of viable alternative to modern-day medicine. If it cannot be detected through the five senses, then it doesn't exist. The world wants proof but is unwilling to go through the processes necessary to obtain that proof for itself. So is it really about scepticism and lack of trust? Or is it about fear? Fear of accountability, fear of admitting they may have been wrong, fear of having to trust in someone that they cannot touch or see. **Ps 53** *"¹The fool has said in his heart, 'There is no God.' They are corrupt, and have done abominable iniquity; There is none who does good."*

Advances recently made among physicists can help us understand a little better how God does in fact carry out miraculous healing. There was a time when scientists thought that the smallest element of matter was atoms. Then they discovered this couldn't be the case because even atoms are divided according to their relevant properties. For instance, the atoms that make up a bird are very different to those that make up a piece of gold. So they split the atom and discovered protons and neutrons. Dis-similar properties were reduced but they still existed. To date, the latest breakthrough is the discovery of quarks, as protons and neutrons seem to break down into tiny flashes of pure energy that constantly pulsate in an irregular fashion that make closer examination very difficult. I understand new machines are being designed to make that closer examination possible.

Ac 17 *"²⁸for in Him we live and move and have our being,"*

So there you have it, the building material, or matter, from which everything has been created appears to be energy. That includes the rocks in your garden, your children and the air that you breathe. There are unbelievably powerful forces that hold these properties together. For instance, wood will always be wood. You can grow and harvest the tree, use the wood to build a cabinet, crush it and then burn it. In every stage of its existence, it will never change from being

Personal Notes

No doubt, you will have encountered in the media the issue of medical ethics. When confronted with sickness and disease for which there is no known secular cure, some people will go to extraordinary lengths to find a remedy rather than confront the cause.

This has resulted in attempts to clone human beings to enable harvesting of their organs. Spinal injuries, Althzeimer's disease, brainstem disfunction; all will be curable in time say the experts. But, to achieve this, they are forced into extending the bounds of common sense and reason into uncharted territory. The result has been cruel and unusual experimentation on animals and some unwilling humans.

Now do you see why it is so important for the whole church to rediscover and apply the healing promises of God and to share that good news with the whole earth. "Repentance brings healing!"

Could you go to the established medical authorities of your Country with that message without first backing it up with real life examples? What do you think? What part can you play?

Please write down what you and your church could do.

wood – unless the Creator interrupts and turns a wooden staff into a snake, which He did for Moses.

No-one can change the properties of matter at a sub-atomic level except the One who controls it. **Jn 1** *"¹In the beginning was the Word, and the Word was with God, and the Word was God. ²He was in the beginning with God. ³All things were made through Him, and without Him nothing was made that was made. ⁴In Him was life, and the life was the light of men."*

When the laws of sin and death are operating and someone gets sick, cellular reorientation is a common cause. For instance, most of us have cells in our body that are potentially harmful, but they're also dormant (or inactive), until something happens that seems to switch them on. A tumour begins to grow and its cells replicate at a frightening rate. Geneticists are keen to find out what causes these cells to switch on and frustrate that process by interfering with the genetic code. Let me give you an analogy of what this means: the electrical system in your house is pre-wired, you are worried that it might short out at some point in the future, so you fit additional fuses into the wiring system to . . . prevent this from happening? Not a chance! You can manipulate the system all you want, but you cannot change the laws that govern how electricity works, which is effectively what they are trying to do with manipulation of the genetic code. **Ps 139** *"¹³For You formed my inward parts; You covered me in my mother's womb. ¹⁴I will praise You, for I am fearfully and wonderfully made; Marvellous are Your works, And that my soul knows very well. ¹⁵My frame was not hidden from You, When I was made in secret, And skilfully wrought in the lowest parts of the earth."*

If you are suffering from a growing tumour and you're asking for divine intervention then God will move at a sub-atomic level to switch off the cancerous cells, which will stop them duplicating (or growing), activate the cells that will effectively "eat" the tumour that has developed thus far and determine the speed at which this happens, which could be over a period of months or seconds.

Personal Notes

No doubt, you will have encountered in the media the issue of medical ethics. When confronted with sickness and disease for which there is no known secular cure, some people will go to extraordinary lengths to find a remedy rather than confront the cause.

This has resulted in attempts to clone human beings to enable harvesting of their organs. Spinal injuries, Althzeimer's disease, brainstem disfunction; all will be curable in time say the experts. But, to achieve this, they are forced into extending the bounds of common sense and reason into uncharted territory. The result has been cruel and unusual experimentation on animals and some unwilling humans.

Now do you see why it is so important for the whole church to rediscover and apply the healing promises of God and to share that good news with the whole earth. "Repentance brings healing!"

Could you go to the established medical authorities of your Country with that message without first backing it up with real life examples? What do you think? What part can you play?

Please write down what you and your church could do.

Suppose your leg has been cut off. Can you grow a new leg? Well, think about it. How did you get your legs in the first place? When your body was being formed in your mother's womb, you did not start out with legs. Those cells programmed to duplicate the bones, sinew and skin that would provide you with legs are still alive and well. Just because you've never seen it happen does not make it impossible. The only problem is, the cellular growth rate can only go so far (full growth) and then it switches off automatically. To reactivate that process (or re-program the cellular code) is beyond the reach of humanity, you must ask the Creator for that to happen and He will decide when, where, how and in what way he will respond to your need.

A surgeon heals by going into the body from the outside, or a doctor may prescribe pills that may ease your condition. Many of these medications, including surgery, can and do have side effects. The analogy of using a sledgehammer to crack a nut is appropriate here, because human medical personnel cannot heal a pre-existing condition at a sub-atomic level. They work at a level way above that, which means this can have an unintended distressing effect on other parts of the body which are often not discovered until the damage has already been done. In all matters of relief from distress, no matter what form they take, God's way is best and all humanity must learn that lesson.

Mk 5 "*25Now a certain woman had a flow of blood for twelve years, 26and had suffered many things from many physicians. She had spent all that she had and was no better, but rather grew worse. 27When she heard about Jesus, she came behind Him in the crowd and touched His garment. 28For she said, 'If only I may touch His clothes, I shall be made well.' 29Immediately the fountain of her blood was dried up, and she felt in her body that she was healed of the affliction. 30And Jesus, immediately knowing in Himself that power had gone out of Him, turned around in the crowd and said, 'Who touched My clothes?' 31But His disciples said to Him, 'You see the multitude thronging You, and You say, Who touched Me?' 32And He looked around to see her who had done this thing. 33But the woman, fearing and trembling, knowing what had happened to her, came and fell down*

Personal Notes

No doubt, you will have encountered in the media the issue of medical ethics. When confronted with sickness and disease for which there is no known secular cure, some people will go to extraordinary lengths to find a remedy rather than confront the cause.

This has resulted in attempts to clone human beings to enable harvesting of their organs. Spinal injuries, Althzeimer's disease, brainstem disfunction; all will be curable in time say the experts. But, to achieve this, they are forced into extending the bounds of common sense and reason into uncharted territory. The result has been cruel and unusual experimentation on animals and some unwilling humans.

Now do you see why it is so important for the whole church to rediscover and apply the healing promises of God and to share that good news with the whole earth. "Repentance brings healing!"

Could you go to the established medical authorities of your Country with that message without first backing it up with real life examples? What do you think? What part can you play?

Please write down what you and your church could do.

before Him and told Him the whole truth. ³⁴*And He said to her, 'Daughter, your faith has made you well. Go in peace, and be healed of your affliction'."*

Sometimes, before Jesus would heal someone, he would ask them, "Do you believe that I am able to do this?" In other words, "Do you recognise my authority over the physical and spiritual world? Do you know who I really am?"

Faith is rock solid belief that what God says He will do, He will do, before you have seen it happen! **Heb 11** *"*¹*Now faith is the substance of things hoped for, the evidence of things not seen."* That faith is a spiritual gift. You cannot conjure it up from your own resources. It must be given before you can receive anything from God!

All human beings are first and foremost spirit beings. We are given a soul which is physical life, self awareness and the five senses which are all moulded into an external apparatus that we call our bodies. The human spirit enters the soul of a baby at the time it is born and separated from its mother by the cutting of the umbilical cord and begins to breathe on its own. (**Gen 2** *"*⁷*And the Lord God formed man of the dust of the ground, and breathed into his nostrils the breath of life; and man became a living being."*) But the human spirit in all human beings, from the youngest to the oldest, is in a distressed condition because we are all separated from our spiritual Father because of sin. Born-again believers have that relationship restored because Christ paid all the penalties of sin (which include sickness and disease) for us.

The new covenant sets the boundaries for that relationship. It is unique, special and should be more highly valued than anything you have in this life, including human life itself.

There is nothing impossible with God. (**Luke 1:37**) Seek to better understand your Father. Jesus said, "Anyone who has seen me, has seen the Father." (**John 14:9**) Look at Jesus' life, what he thought, how he lived, how he treated others. Learn to think as he thinks. View the world through his eyes.

Personal Notes

No doubt, you will have encountered in the media the issue of medical ethics. When confronted with sickness and disease for which there is no known secular cure, some people will go to extraordinary lengths to find a remedy rather than confront the cause.

This has resulted in attempts to clone human beings to enable harvesting of their organs. Spinal injuries, Althzeimer's disease, brainstem disfunction; all will be curable in time say the experts. But, to achieve this, they are forced into extending the bounds of common sense and reason into uncharted territory. The result has been cruel and unusual experimentation on animals and some unwilling humans.

Now do you see why it is so important for the whole church to rediscover and apply the healing promises of God and to share that good news with the whole earth. "Repentance brings healing!"

Could you go to the established medical authorities of your Country with that message without first backing it up with real life examples? What do you think? What part can you play?

Please write down what you and your church could do.

In any and every situation, always ask, "What would Christ have me do? What would He do?"

Then happily accept the extraordinary grace, blessing and joy of being a member of the God family and cherish your future eternal inheritance.

Finally, be prepared to be a consistent conduit of blessing from the Father, through Jesus Christ, through you, to everybody else!

CHAPTER NINE

From Asking to Deliverance – A Time of Testing!

For the umpteenth time, I emphasise that this process of waiting applies only to Christians and this process cannot be hurried. God is waiting for alignment to occur. You are at point A, but your deliverance is over at point B. You cannot get there by yourself, you need to be led and that means total submission and reliance upon God. Be very careful to listen, follow every insight, seek reconciliation in every relationship. Be constant in prayer for the work, repent of every sin and tell everyone who asks that God will deliver you. Read your personal notes in this book. Are you acting on what you've been led to do? Search the scriptures and obey the commands of your Saviour.

During this period of waiting, some will feel led to seek medical assistance. That's absolutely fine; but do not be tempted to use medical relief as a means to avoid the growth that is being demanded of you. You must still go through the same process as those who don't.

Watch what you say and even think. Avoid self-condemnation! Life and death are in the power of the tongue (**James 3**) and what is spoken-out can be made to come to pass. (**Mat 10:36,37**) One of the greatest temptations faced by *all* Christians, when going through this process, is self pity. I cannot emphasise enough how dangerous this is. What kind of example are you setting if, after going through the corrective process, knowing that your healing is on its way, you then think you can bring glory to God by putting on the face of a constipated camel?

Wash your face, do your hair, put on your best and finest clothes. Greet everyone with a smile that radiates pure joy and when they ask in that simpering tone, "I'm sorry to hear about your trial, what do the doctors say?" Tell them loudly and firmly, "I have been healed by Jesus Christ himself. I am waiting for the physical manifestation of that healing in my body which shall happen at the appointed time, but I give thanks every day, in great expectation of that day of deliverance!" (**Rom 4:17**) At this point they will quietly excuse themselves and go talk to somebody else. Some will say, "Hallelujah" and rejoice with you, but don't expect too many of them.

When you say something like that God listens. The angels stop and pay heed, even the demons shrink back. The spirit world pays attention and carnally-minded people will withdraw themselves from you. **Eph 6** "*10Finally, my brethren, be strong in the Lord and in the power of His might. 11Put on the whole armor of God, that you may be able to stand against the wiles of the devil. 12For we do not wrestle against flesh and blood, but against principalities, against powers, against the rulers of the darkness of this age, against spiritual hosts of wickedness in the heavenly places. 13Therefore take up the whole armor of God, that you may be able to withstand in the evil day, and having done all, to stand. 14Stand therefore, having girded your waist with truth, having put on the breastplate of righteousness, 15and having shod your feet with the preparation of the gospel of peace; 16above all, taking the shield of faith with which you will be able to quench all the fiery darts of the wicked one. 17And take the helmet of salvation, and the sword of the Spirit, which is the Word of God; 18praying always with all prayer and supplication in the Spirit, being watchful to this end with all perseverance and supplication for all the saints.*"

Self-pity only brings with it self-condemnation, depression and ultimately despair – the conviction that everything is pointless so you just want to give up. Let me tell you something: once or twice I've been there. No effort is required to give-in to this feeling.

Personal Notes

Congratulations!

Your faithful adherence to what has been revealed through the Holy Spirit and the Word of God has led to your deliverance. What has happened to you will be of enormous encouragement to everyone who knows you.

Don't forget, first, you receive in the Spirit, then your healing is manifested to everyone when it appears in the flesh.

It will happen any day now. It could happen in your home when you wake up in the morning. It could happen at a church meeting or through an evangelist presenter on television.

Let us know when it does. Your shared testimony will help thousands. Keep making notes of what takes place and when.

Your body welcomes it, your mind readily accepts it, there is almost a peace to it. There is a scripture that says, "The kingdom of heaven belongs to the violent and the violent shall take it by force!" To all these thoughts and feelings, you shout no! There is a time to fight and this is it. You pull out every scripture that confirms who you are in Christ. You go before your Father and you tell Him that you're under attack and remind Him of His promises of supernatural protection. You tell Him that you have chosen Christ of your own free will and that you do not recognise the right of Satan to attack you and that you demand that he be restrained so that you can stay in your Father's perfect will.

I know, I know. It sounds almost disrespectful. You can imagine religious-minded people saying, "How dare you talk to God like that?" Well, I have done it and I have not been struck by a bolt of lightning. Instead, deliverance from that self-pity has come instantaneously. The feeling of relief is incredible. You feel lighter, freer and happier; *and* you feel so strong and powerful. It's almost as if nothing can possibly harm you. God is no respecter of persons. What He has done for me, He will do for you also.

Make no mistake, this is a choice of who you choose to serve. Will it be Christ the King, or Satan the destroyer. To serve Christ, read and sing the Psalms, reject despairing thoughts, confess who you are in Christ and deny the power of sin and sickness over your life and declare victory as a matter of faith before you've even received it.

You are in a fight and these mind battles are making you stronger. Be filled with righteous anger when you feel tempted and speak out loud the sword of truth (scriptures) to defeat the weakening thoughts and prods of Satan.

Incremental relief is a valid prayer request. The Christian family, in general, does know about this. While you are in your weakened state, waiting for the day of deliverance, you will come across "wrinkles". These are little twists of the knife that are added to disrupt your confident expectation. They can come in the form of: additional

Personal Notes

Congratulations!

Your faithful adherence to what has been revealed through the Holy Spirit and the Word of God has led to your deliverance. What has happened to you will be of enormous encouragement to everyone who knows you.

Don't forget, first, you receive in the Spirit, then your healing is manifested to everyone when it appears in the flesh.

It will happen any day now. It could happen in your home when you wake up in the morning. It could happen at a church meeting or through an evangelist presenter on television.

Let us know when it does. Your shared testimony will help thousands. Keep making notes of what takes place and when.

bad news that your condition has worsened, physical pain in an area that wasn't there before, a new financial or relationship problem or some other form of bad news, or even some kind of threat.

We are authorised by the Word of God to seek immediate relief when these wrinkles occur. **Mt 6** *"¹¹Give us this day our daily bread. ³⁴Therefore do not worry about tomorrow, for tomorrow will worry about its own things. Sufficient for the day is its own trouble."* **Php 4** *"⁶Be anxious for nothing, but in everything by prayer and supplication, with thanksgiving, let your requests be made known to God."* Please understand, your faithful struggle is taking place while you are in a very weakened state and Satan will kick you while you are down! Your day of deliverance is still not here yet, but this added suffering can be dealt with immediately.

To help illustrate this point, let me tell you what happened when I became convicted of the need to write this book. I knew I was going to need a personal example of deliverance to help validate this text in the eyes of doubters. In addition, the authority of this book and the scriptures from which that authority is drawn would have to be tested in the life of an unrelated believer, and the final test would be divine intervention in the life of a non-believer.

To deal with the first test, I agreed with our heavenly Father that the next time I was assailed with a health problem, I was not going to seek any form of relief except from God Himself, unless He authorised otherwise.

I didn't have long to wait. While I was still compiling notes for this book and constantly seeking wisdom and inspiration, a recent tooth repair disintegrated leaving a cavity. I have always had weak teeth and dental work has made little difference in slowing the process of decay. So my future witness was now being established. I went before God and asked for complete restoration and healing of my teeth, including the replacement of those already lost. Ever heard of that before? No, nor have I.

Personal Notes

Congratulations!

Your faithful adherence to what has been revealed through the Holy Spirit and the Word of God has led to your deliverance. What has happened to you will be of enormous encouragement to everyone who knows you.

Don't forget, first, you receive in the Spirit, then your healing is manifested to everyone when it appears in the flesh.

It will happen any day now. It could happen in your home when you wake up in the morning. It could happen at a church meeting or through an evangelist presenter on television.

Let us know when it does. Your shared testimony will help thousands. Keep making notes of what takes place and when.

That was nearly two years ago and I am still waiting. Anyway, a few months after this request was made, the decay got worse as two other teeth began to fall apart – and that was when it happened!

One evening, as I was eating dinner, a nerve in one of the decayed teeth suddenly became exposed, I nearly jumped through the ceiling. The pain was absolutely unbelievable. I rushed to the bathroom and splashed cold water into my mouth, to no avail. Then I tried warm water which brought slight relief, then the pain returned with a vengeance. I kid you not, if I had had access to a gun I would have blown my head clean off.

In my bedside cabinet, I had one of those temporary dental repair kits. I pulled it out and then stopped. I suddenly realised this was it. I was going to have to rely on pure faith to get me through this. The only way to make this book come alive was to reject this medical option and ask for immediate relief.

I couldn't think clearly. I rocked back and forth on my bed. How on earth do you pray when the pain is so devastatingly real. I can't remember everything I said, but it was along the lines of: "Father, please help me, this is killing me. I don't want to use the medical option, which will defeat the whole purpose of the book I'm writing, . . . Oh God, *stop the pain*. I know you are the Creator. You made the nervous system to alert the brain when the body is damaged. So it's done its job. I'm aware my teeth need attention, so please switch the nerves off!"

Although I could hardly believe it, the pain was definitely beginning to recede. I put the dental repair kit back in the drawer and walked shakily back to the living room.

My nerves were shattered. Was the pain going to come back? I was careful not to make any sudden movements. Oops! Was that a slight twinge? No, no, the pain had gone away. At the end of that evening, I gave the most prolific, most thankful prayer of praise of my entire Christian life. I was assured in the Spirit, that so long as I remained

Personal Notes

Congratulations!

Your faithful adherence to what has been revealed through the Holy Spirit and the Word of God has led to your deliverance. What has happened to you will be of enormous encouragement to everyone who knows you.

Don't forget, first, you receive in the Spirit, then your healing is manifested to everyone when it appears in the flesh.

It will happen any day now. It could happen in your home when you wake up in the morning. It could happen at a church meeting or through an evangelist presenter on television.

Let us know when it does. Your shared testimony will help thousands. Keep making notes of what takes place and when.

faithful in doing what God had given me to do, I would have nothing to worry about concerning the return of that pain.

There has been some additional deterioration of my teeth; but it's very slight. The pain has never returned in nearly eighteen months. Once this book is finished, I believe that God wants me to go and visit my dentist, but only for an X-ray. Doubtless, the dentist will prevail upon me to let him fix my teeth and that's when I will tell him that Jesus Christ is taking care of that for me. I will then inform him that I will return once I have received my new teeth and allow him to take another X-ray, for a witness!

God communicates the gospel through His Word and also through us. We are like little Christs representing the kingdom of God on earth. Living witnesses of how life was intended to be. Some Christian leaders have made disparaging remarks about the so-called health and wealth gospel. Some of their criticisms are valid, but much of it is not. We have all been called to live an abundant life in Christ Jesus. He desires that we should prosper in every area of life: in our relationships, in wisdom and understanding, in our health, in our work, in everything.

Very soon, you are going to be healed. Maybe, in direct contrast to what your local church believes. God will use you to change that. He wants His family to agree on these basic principles and be prepared to help each other out, learn from each other, cooperate with each other. The strength of one denomination may be in the area of prophecy, in another, counselling, in another, overseas evangelism. These gifts are given to serve the whole body, not just one group of churches.

Jesus Christ is coming back very, very soon. Probably in our lifetime. Now that you've been healed, use this second chance to devote the rest of your life to the promotion of the gospel in whatever area or gift he has given you.

Now I have a personal request. God is leading me to set up a free website that will showcase letters from believers such as yourself

Personal Notes

Congratulations!

Your faithful adherence to what has been revealed through the Holy Spirit and the Word of God has led to your deliverance. What has happened to you will be of enormous encouragement to everyone who knows you.

Don't forget, first, you receive in the Spirit, then your healing is manifested to everyone when it appears in the flesh.

It will happen any day now. It could happen in your home when you wake up in the morning. It could happen at a church meeting or through an evangelist presenter on television.

Let us know when it does. Your shared testimony will help thousands. Keep making notes of what takes place and when.

who have been miraculously delivered from a difficult trial. For the sake of your brethren, I am asking you to send an e-mail, of up to 250 words setting-out the problem you faced, the main areas God corrected you on and how He brought deliverance. Include a contact e-mail or phone number, so that someone similarly affected can contact you and you can partner with them. Thank you.

Note: The first three testimonies on this website will be myself, a fellow believer and an unbeliever who receives a witness of the gospel for the first time and is instantly healed. Details about the website are given at the end of this book.

CHAPTER TEN

The Warning of a Cleaned Room!

The whole basis and strength of demonic power is disobedience. Rebellion, or the refusal to acknowledge and obey, is the very definition of witchcraft. Anyone who has been "cleaned" of demonic influence or possession can be entrapped again if they do not accept the Lordship of Christ in their lives.

Demonic powers are restless spirits that have made their home among certain people. Once they have been cast out, they don't like it and will seek to return to what they consider is their rightful home. **Mt 12** *"43When an unclean spirit goes out of a man, he goes through dry places, seeking rest, and finds none. 44Then he says, 'I will return to my house from which I came.' And when he comes, he finds it empty, swept, and put in order. 45Then he goes and takes with him seven other spirits more wicked than himself, and they enter and dwell there; and the last state of that man is worse than the first. So shall it also be with this wicked generation."* It is not enough to be delivered from demonic influence. The void has to be filled by something else.

Anyone, even a Christian, who has been delivered from any kind of affliction, must keep in mind the lessons learned from their experience and not return to the former way of thinking, speaking or doing. To do so, will open the door for demonic influence to re-enter that life, often with much worse consequences than before.

All of God's people who belong to Him and have the Holy Spirit and whose names are written in the Lamb's book of life are known to those who dwell in the spirit realm. This includes the angels and the demons. In the spirit realm we stand out like a sore thumb. What is also known is the extent of our talents, gifts and authority. If someone stands up and proclaims that they are a teacher of the Word and they have the gifts and talents to teach *but have not been authorised.* Then those same teachers can be misled, deceived and used by evil spirits to bring deception upon those being taught. **2 Pe 2** *"¹But there were also false prophets among the people, even as there will be false teachers among you, who will secretly bring in destructive heresies, even denying the Lord who bought them, and bring on themselves swift destruction."*

Authority is the key to everything. Man can promote you all the way up to being king over the whole earth, but that doesn't mean you have God-given authority. Jesus Christ was not much to look at as a physical man. In many ways he was very ordinary and difficult to pick out from among even a small group of men. But how many times was he confronted by a demon-possessed person who saw his spiritual persona? **Mk 1** *"²³Now there was a man in their synagogue with an unclean spirit. And he cried out, ²⁴saying, 'Let us alone! What have we to do with You, Jesus of Nazareth? Did You come to destroy us? I know who You are – the Holy One of God!' ²⁵But Jesus rebuked him, saying, 'Be quiet, and come out of him!' ²⁶And when the unclean spirit had convulsed him and cried out with a loud voice, he came out of him. ²⁷Then they were all amazed, so that they questioned among themselves, saying, 'What is this? What new doctrine is this? For with authority He commands even the unclean spirits, and they obey Him.' ²⁸And immediately His fame spread throughout all the region around Galilee."* That demon knew he was in the presence of incredible power and great authority. One word from Jesus was all it took to send this demon packing.

Authority is not something that can be adopted or taken, it must be conferred. In the body of Christ there are many believers in various denominations with differing gifts and talents, at various stages of spiritual growth. You may well be anointed for a particular calling

Personal Notes

Now is not the time to let down your guard. I have seen this happen to so many Christians: they walk the path to deliverance only to allow their conduct to return to what it was. They don't press forward into the new life that God has prepared for them and, before you know it, they are once more back under personal bondage.

Take care not to lose this book. Commit yourself to review the whole book, especially your personal notes, every month. Keep re-reading the scriptures quoted until they are a part of your thinking.

Use this chapter's personal notes section to add new insights that occur to you from your monthly reviews. Don't allow anything to "mess up" your clean room.

with a special mission, but you will not receive that "special authority" until you're deemed ready.

David was anointed to be king over Israel. Many people knew it and encouraged him to claim his inheritance, even take it by force. However, David was wise enough to wait until the time decreed by God Himself when he would receive divine favour and power that would accompany that legitimate authority.

So what happens to those who claim to have Godly authority to do a particular thing, but actually don't? **Dt 18** *"20But the prophet who presumes to speak a word in My name, which I have not commanded him to speak, or who speaks in the name of other gods, that prophet shall die."*

In the book of **Acts, chapter 19** some Jewish exorcists tried to replicate the work of the disciples by calling on the name of Jesus to cast out an evil spirit. The spirit did not recognise their authority (because they never really had it in the first place) and assaulted them with such violence they were lucky to escape with their lives. **Ac 19** *"13Then some of the itinerant Jewish exorcists took it upon themselves to call the name of the Lord Jesus over those who had evil spirits, saying, 'We exorcise you by the Jesus whom Paul preaches.' 14Also there were seven sons of Sceva, a Jewish chief priest, who did so. 15And the evil spirit answered and said, 'Jesus I know, and Paul I know; but who are you?' 16Then the man in whom the evil spirit was leaped on them, overpowered them, and prevailed against them, so that they fled out of that house naked and wounded."*

Sometimes, church members in different parts of the world, decide to start a new ministry or join a pressure group or seek to evangelise a section of the community encountering terrible hardship and suffering as a result. The most common explanation given is that this is a normal part of life for those bringing the gospel to unbelievers. In turn, those unbelievers who choose to respond and make a commitment suddenly find themselves being violently oppressed and an example is made of them to the wider community. As a result, the

Personal Notes

Now is not the time to let down your guard. I have seen this happen to so many Christians: they walk the path to deliverance only to allow their conduct to return to what it was. They don't press forward into the new life that God has prepared for them and, before you know it, they are once more back under personal bondage.

Take care not to lose this book. Commit yourself to review the whole book, especially your personal notes, every month. Keep re-reading the scriptures quoted until they are a part of your thinking.

Use this chapter's personal notes section to add new insights that occur to you from your monthly reviews. Don't allow anything to "mess up" your clean room.

fledgling work is shut down and fear and oppression in that community becomes more further entrenched than it was before.

Yes, we do encounter opposition. Yes, there may be attempts to repress the gospel in these areas, but if God Himself has sanctioned this move He will cause events and people to cooperate. He will bring divine protection, favour and healing into their midst and no-one will be able to withstand Him. But those He sends will be sent with the authority they need to complete the task successfully. Some Christian leaders try to sow into soil that is not yet ready for them and this can lead to chaos, even disaster – not just for them, but for the very people they were trying to help. We have to keep reminding ourselves, "This is not my work; this is God's work!"

In another set of circumstances, you may be authorised to do a certain thing but, after a while, it doesn't appear to be yielding the kind of results you are used to. There is a common cause for this type of situation. A well-documented incident in the gospels (**Matthew 17**) illustrates this. The disciples sought to heal a demon-possessed boy and, for some reason, they couldn't do it. They went to Jesus who immediately healed the boy and then rebuked them because of their unbelief. He then appears to instruct them to fast and pray the next time they're confronted with a demonic spirit that resists them. Why? So as to force God to do what they want? No, absolutely not. The disciples had the authority, yet they were resisted. Other scriptures suggest the disciples were starting to get a little above themselves. Some of their human nature was beginning to intrude on their divine duties. Pride was in the air, "Hey, look at us! See what we can do!" Praying and fasting would have put paid to that emerging attitude of cockiness and one-upmanship. Humility would have been restored and faith along with it.

Pride is such a tricky thing. You can have pride and not even know it. **Jer 17** "*9The heart is deceitful above all things, And desperately wicked; Who can know it?*" Self deception is possibly our greatest enemy which is why, whenever we review scripture or, hear messages concerning the status of our spiritual condition, we should do so with an

Personal Notes

Now is not the time to let down your guard. I have seen this happen to so many Christians: they walk the path to deliverance only to allow their conduct to return to what it was. They don't press forward into the new life that God has prepared for them and, before you know it, they are once more back under personal bondage.

Take care not to lose this book. Commit yourself to review the whole book, especially your personal notes, every month. Keep re-reading the scriptures quoted until they are a part of your thinking.

Use this chapter's personal notes section to add new insights that occur to you from your monthly reviews. Don't allow anything to "mess up" your clean room.

attitude of self-correction. **2 Pet 1** *"⁵But also for this very reason, giving all diligence, add to your faith virtue, to virtue knowledge, ⁶to knowledge self-control, to self-control perseverance, to perseverance godliness, ⁷to godliness brotherly kindness, and to brotherly kindness love. ⁸For if these things are yours and abound, you will be neither barren nor unfruitful in the knowledge of our Lord Jesus Christ. ⁹For he who lacks these things is shortsighted, even to blindness, and has forgotten that he was cleansed from his old sins. ¹⁰Therefore, brethren, be even more diligent to make your call and election sure, for if you do these things you will never stumble; ¹¹for so an entrance will be supplied to you abundantly into the everlasting kingdom of our Lord and Saviour Jesus Christ."* Any attempt to justify behaviour or, a way of thinking that is clearly shown to be in error, will ultimately render you deaf and blind. If that happens, you will find the only way that God can get your attention is to use a big stick. Why would anyone deliberately choose that?

The purpose of this chapter is to prepare you for the last two chapters of this book. Having received divine intervention in your circumstances, your "cleaned" state is strictly temporary. You must now follow through on what God has shown you to do. Be wary of compromise and distraction. There's plenty of it in this world. Support, both financially and in prayer, the type of ministry (area of service) that God is leading you toward. Increase your knowledge and understanding in that specific area. Get to know some of the people already operating in that area and be ready to lend assistance whenever it's asked for.

Note: You will become more aware of other people's mistakes. Particularly those who are in authority in that area of ministry. Do not fall into the trap of criticising them. Offer new options they might wish to consider but remain respectful at all times. Don't get impatient. You might wish to try one or two things on your own, but always get permission first. God never undermines an originally conferred authority. You may receive wisdom and insight that takes you beyond the current thinking in that particular ministry. Well, trust me, this is yet another test to see how you respond and whether

Personal Notes

Now is not the time to let down your guard. I have seen this happen to so many Christians: they walk the path to deliverance only to allow their conduct to return to what it was. They don't press forward into the new life that God has prepared for them and, before you know it, they are once more back under personal bondage.

Take care not to lose this book. Commit yourself to review the whole book, especially your personal notes, every month. Keep re-reading the scriptures quoted until they are a part of your thinking.

Use this chapter's personal notes section to add new insights that occur to you from your monthly reviews. Don't allow anything to "mess up" your clean room.

or not you can be trusted not to interfere with the current divine order of things.

You will get the opportunity to do small things at first. Your faithfulness in these seemingly unimportant areas will yield the greater challenges later.

What about your job? That may have to change, especially if the responsibilities that go with it threaten the new life that God is leading you toward. You may be a good accountant but the world is full of good accountants. Your future area of service is unique because of its scarcity. There may be very few other people doing what you've been called to do. Also, if your current job is not utilising what you know are major talents and interests in your life that could best be used within the work of God then you should be ready for a major change. But test the spirits yourself. **1 Jn 4** *"¹Beloved, do not believe every spirit, but test the spirits, whether they are of God; because many false prophets have gone out into the world."* If you are leaning towards a decision that could have a major impact on your economic well-being, seek wise counsel from those who have already done it. Ask God to confirm His will to you by some unmistakable means.

You'll probably find your relationships will also change. Lifelong friendships may need to be abandoned or, estranged relationships reacquainted. You may be required to relocate to a new area, or maybe even to a new church (although this is rare). You might even have to move to a new Country.

God is taking you to a higher level of faith and service, so it would be wise to expect at least some opposition. Do not be amazed when it appears to come from those you considered to be your best friends or even from relatives.

Remember, everything is a test. From the smallest events to the greatest you are being evaluated and judged. How you react to these changes, to these irritants, even to radical new blessings, will determine the point at which you enter your predestined area of authority.

Personal Notes

Now is not the time to let down your guard. I have seen this happen to so many Christians: they walk the path to deliverance only to allow their conduct to return to what it was. They don't press forward into the new life that God has prepared for them and, before you know it, they are once more back under personal bondage.

Take care not to lose this book. Commit yourself to review the whole book, especially your personal notes, every month. Keep re-reading the scriptures quoted until they are a part of your thinking.

Use this chapter's personal notes section to add new insights that occur to you from your monthly reviews. Don't allow anything to "mess up" your clean room.

Be especially wary of losing your temper or making decisions that could distract you from where you're being led. Your Father is getting set to entrust you with greater responsibility than you've ever had before and the power and authority that goes with it. Make sure your relationship with Him has the absolute highest priority and, please, never hesitate to ask for wisdom, read **Proverbs 2**. Expect it and cherish it when it comes.

There is great power in a partnership. Every David needs his Jonathan, every Mary needs her Elizabeth. You are greatly blessed if that partner is your spouse, but if not God will bring you someone you can really trust as both a prayer and ministry partner.

As you fill your cleaned room with new things, the personal vision that God has set aside for you will become ever clearer. Your security in Christ will greatly increase and so will your prominence among the unbelievers. You are a light on a hill and as the days we live in become ever darker, you are going to stand out more and more. Don't fear it, embrace it, for it was to this that you were first called.

CHAPTER ELEVEN

Are We Really Empowered to Heal Others?

It's a mind-boggling question, isn't it? When I first began to realise the truth about divine healing, I was terrified at the prospect. One man of faith versus thousands of medical professionals all saying that to re-enact the same miracles Christ performed when he was on the earth is impossible.

So the question is, "Do we have the power and authority to do this? **Mk 16** "*¹⁷And these signs will follow those who believe: In My name they will cast out demons; they will speak with new tongues; ¹⁸they will take up serpents; and if they drink anything deadly, it will by no means hurt them; they will lay hands on the sick, and they will recover.*" When we, as Christians, need healing there is a process we have to go through; but what about everybody else? What about those who ask you if you'll help them and then as you lay hands on them they're healed straight away or within the hour? Who really has the faith to do that?

To answer all these questions, we must begin by recognising who we are. When you look in the mirror, you may not be all that impressed by what you see. But your physical body, your age, your appearance, even your personality does not accurately reflect where you stand in the spirit realm.

We are described by God as His children. That means we inherit many of His characteristics. But we are not yet eternal beings as He is. We are not yet self-existing, as He is. We are described as the royal household of God, as kings and priests. Do your friends and relatives see you that way? They would probably laugh themselves silly if you went around describing yourself like that. **1 Pet 2** "*5you also, as living stones, are being built up a spiritual house, a holy priesthood, to offer up spiritual sacrifices acceptable to God through Jesus Christ. 9But you are a chosen generation, a royal priesthood, a holy nation, His own special people, that you may proclaim the praises of Him who called you out of darkness into His marvelous light; 12having your conduct honorable among the Gentiles, that when they speak against you as evildoers, they may, by your good works which they observe, glorify God in the day of visitation.*"

Let me try and illustrate what happened to you and me when each of us became one of the "Chosen Ones": One morning, there is a knock at your door. You answer it to find someone standing there who identifies himself as "the King's messenger". He hands you an envelope that has the royal insignia on it and it has your name emblazoned on it in pure gold. You go inside and carefully open the letter and this is what it says:

Dear [your name appears here]

I am pleased to inform you that as a result of the heavenly decree of the new covenant, you have been chosen for adoption into the royal family of God. As a consequence of adoption, it has been decreed that you will share a joint inheritance with the Prince of Peace, Jesus, the Christ. As a member of His family, you will be given exclusive access to the very throne of God the Father, to make petitions on your own behalf and on behalf of others.

Your royal duties include full participation in the family business which will require you to declare the gospel of Jesus Christ to all nations throughout the world. You, along with other faithful members of our family, will be given everything you need to complete your assignment, including the power, demonstrated through Jesus Christ (your older brother), to heal the sick, cast out demons and raise the dead.

You will be given a personal bodyguard and supernatural gifts to help you fulfil your assignment. Once completed, you

Personal Notes

Dare to believe what Christ is telling you!

In addition to the exercise you are encouraged to do at the end of this chapter, write your personal vision, of intercession by God, for someone you care about. Write down the person's name, what you know of their circumstances, what personal, physical help and visitation you can offer them and conclude with a statement of what you intend to say to them about what God can and will do for them.

Finally, commit the whole scenario to earnest, believing prayer. You'll be amazed at what happens next.

will ascend to the heavenly realm to begin your new life in the glory of eternity.

All the above is true. It is right there in scripture. Of course, while we remain in the flesh, this can seem like a fairy tale. You might ask, "What was so special about me that I should be 'chosen'?" Well, the answer is not exactly a boost to our ego: Jesus says, "The weak and the foolish of this world have been chosen to put to shame and confound the wisdom of the mighty." So there you have it: "Weak and Foolish", That's you and me.

Whatever progress we make in our lives, whatever we do right, whatever noble virtues we appear to acquire, they all come from Jesus Christ, through the power of the Holy Spirit, so that no flesh will ever be able to boast or glorify themselves in His presence.

So in the flesh, we're not much to look at. Before our calling there was little to admire. But in the Spirit realm we have status, wisdom, knowledge and authority.

What do you suppose happens when the daughter of the president of the USA runs into the Oval office in the White House to speak to her father? She gets a personal audience with her dad. Although he may generally be considered the most powerful man in the world, this girl has no qualms about asking her dad for help on the smallest of matters. If she knows of someone who is in distress, she can tell her father about it and, for the sake of his child, he can send help and favour to that person who would otherwise continue in his dilemma. Likewise, when we approach our Heavenly Father about someone in dire straits, for the sake of His child, God will cause that person to receive a witness that will generate the faith needed to receive deliverance from that trouble.

That is the kind of the power you and I have. No one on earth is beyond our help. If you hear about a person, a nation or any kind of situation and are moved by it, tell your heavenly Father about it and

Personal Notes

Dare to believe what Christ is telling you!

In addition to the exercise you are encouraged to do at the end of this chapter, write your personal vision, of intercession by God, for someone you care about. Write down the person's name, what you know of their circumstances, what personal, physical help and visitation you can offer them and conclude with a statement of what you intend to say to them about what God can and will do for them.

Finally, commit the whole scenario to earnest, believing prayer. You'll be amazed at what happens next.

ask Him to send help. Remember, all the other people in this world are potentially future members of your family!

We are called priests of God or empowered intercessors. Jesus says, "Whatsoever you ask the Father in My name will be done for you." (**John 16:23**). We can stop wars, remove kings, bring water to dry lands. All this needs is faith and faith is built on the back of obedience in the small things. **Mt 25** *"²¹His lord said to him, 'Well done, good and faithful servant; you were faithful over a few things, I will make you ruler over many things. Enter into the joy of your lord'."* You cannot have faith to do the big things until you have demonstrated faith in the small things, which is why we need to keep ourselves constantly aware of the commands Jesus gave us in the gospels and literally start living by them.

Can we heal whomever we like, at any given time? For the umpteenth time, let me repeat, this is not our work, this is God's work. He doesn't work for us; we work for Him. This is a little difficult to explain unless you've experienced this but here goes:

The Holy Spirit within us communicates the things of God to us at certain times. One of the ways He does this is by giving what we'll call a "flash of inspiration!", swiftly followed by "certainty!". You live the moment, you are not always prepared beforehand when you go into a situation. This is why Jesus urges us to pray without ceasing, or to keep God at the forefront of our minds all the time. Okay, suppose you feel led to visit a cancer ward at a local hospital one day. You may not know anyone there, but it's visiting time and one of the patients is by herself. You decide to go talk to her. You feel led to declare who you are in Christ and you find she responds very positively. Now what? This is where we can get it wrong – it happened to me once. One of two things is going to have to happen. Either she will suddenly declare her conviction that Jesus will heal her if you ask Him on her behalf . . . in which case, go ahead, you have just been authorised! Or, you will be filled with a rush of extraordinary faith, actual power *and* you will be given the exact words to speak, so go ahead; again you have just been authorised!

142

Personal Notes

Dare to believe what Christ is telling you!

In addition to the exercise you are encouraged to do at the end of this chapter, write your personal vision, of intercession by God, for someone you care about. Write down the person's name, what you know of their circumstances, what personal, physical help and visitation you can offer them and conclude with a statement of what you intend to say to them about what God can and will do for them.

Finally, commit the whole scenario to earnest, believing prayer. You'll be amazed at what happens next.

It is exceptionally rare to know beforehand when, or even who, God is going to heal through you. A faithful servant should be ready at a moment's notice to obey the voice of the Holy Spirit and you cannot be ready unless your relationship with God is truly prospering and you are readily obedient in all the smaller things. Everything Jesus did in the realm of miraculous healing was an example to us. He did nothing of His own power or decision. **Jn 14** *"¹⁰Do you not believe that I am in the Father, and the Father in Me? The words that I speak to you I do not speak on My own authority; but the Father who dwells in Me does the works."* His perfect obedience meant that He heard the Holy Spirit clearly, all the time. The Holy Spirit showed Him who to heal, what to do, and what to say. He was granted supernatural perception so that He could respond to things that were hidden to everybody else. We cannot adequately carry out such an assignment without that same gift and, once again, we come back to the closeness of our relationship to our heavenly Father and the level of our faithfulness and obedience.

It comes and goes doesn't it? You know, sometimes we are so full of faith and feel so close to God that absolutely nothing seems impossible. I have heard of people of faith who have been used supernaturally to heal a sick or dying person and afterward those people seem to just fade away and nobody hears of them again. We do need consistency in our love walk with God and with each other. We also need conviction . . . the absolute belief that God can and will use us in this truly remarkable way.

Therefore, I feel compelled to ask you to do something that you may never have heard of before. Call it an exercise in self-fulfilling prophecy:

I want you to go back and start reading the four gospels again, beginning with **Matthew**. This time, whenever you read an account of Jesus healing someone, or casting out an evil spirit, or raising someone from the dead, I want you to put yourself, not in His position, but in that situation.

Personal Notes

Dare to believe what Christ is telling you!

In addition to the exercise you are encouraged to do at the end of this chapter, write your personal vision, of intercession by God, for someone you care about. Write down the person's name, what you know of their circumstances, what personal, physical help and visitation you can offer them and conclude with a statement of what you intend to say to them about what God can and will do for them.

Finally, commit the whole scenario to earnest, believing prayer. You'll be amazed at what happens next.

For example: In **Luke 5:12**, "A man full of leprosy comes up to *me* and says, 'If Jesus Christ is willing, He will save me and make me clean!' So I tell him, 'Yes Jesus Christ *is* willing. Therefore, by His authority, I command that you be cleaned!' At that point I reach out and touch him and the man is cleansed of leprosy."

Get the idea? Go ahead, do what I ask. This is a real faith-building exercise. Even better, write out each and every incident in the way I've described and visualise each event as it takes place.

This is not blasphemous. Jesus is still doing the healing; it's just that now, He does it through us. You'll be surprised what a difference this will make to your way of thinking and you'll be perfectly prepared for our final chapter.

CHAPTER TWELVE

Now, Heal the Sick, Cast-out Demons and Raise the Dead!

Knowledge and obedience bring faith. Are you ready to do all the above? **Ac 8** *"⁵Then Philip went down to the city of Samaria and preached Christ to them. ⁶And the multitudes with one accord heeded the things spoken by Philip, hearing and seeing the miracles which he did. ⁷For unclean spirits, crying with a loud voice, came out of many who were possessed; and many who were paralyzed and lame were healed. ⁸And there was great joy in that city."* As you read this you may be thinking, "That's not me. I could never do something like that!". Don't worry, your position in the work of God is decided by our Father. You will be gifted with both the will and the means to carry out His instructions, which may not include this part of the work. **Php 2** *"¹³for it is God who works in you both to will and to do for His good pleasure."* **1 Co 7** *"⁷For I wish that all men were even as I myself. But each one has his own gift from God, one in this manner and another in that."* Your responsibility is to find out what you are gifted to do and follow the course you are given.

If you have been inspired on this subject, you should know that the accountability factor is very high and so are the risks. When Paul cast a demon out of a young girl who was bothering him her owners, who were making a tidy profit from her "psychic" abilities, which were now lost, caused Paul and his friend to be brutally beaten and then cast into prison (**Acts 16**). Not everyone is going to appreciate this gift, and if God intends to use you in this way, you are going to be noticed. Your public profile will increase dramatically.

The first disciples who started out as ordinary fishermen became household names because of the miracles that God worked through them. Big symbols make big targets and those often represent a threat to established order. Your life will come under forensic-type scrutiny and any and all means will be used to undermine your work, including false accusations that can have devastating consequences. The way you respond to these challenges shows how accountable you are, and to whom. For example, Paul responded to his dilemma by singing psalms and the prison was turned upside down.

Okay, so all the above was a reality check, but Jesus said, "Be of good cheer for I have overcome the world!" (**John 16:33**) In other words, do not fret and worry yourself. Take each day as it comes and God will provide the abundance for that day in whatever form it needs to take.

Let us take a country such as Rwanda. A few years ago, this nation went through a horrendous experience in which almost half the population slaughtered the other half. Obscene acts of cruelty were committed against men and women, and even on very young children. Rape, torture and other acts of sickening brutality were carried out on a massive scale. In the aftermath of such an event, we are left with the bereaved, the injured, the terrified and vengeance-filled victims on one side and with the perpetrators, racked with guilt, dreading the consequences and totally defensive, on the other.

In Rwanda, some stability has been restored, but there is great grief, great anger and a dreadful thirst for vengeance. Imagine that at this point the Word of God comes to you saying He wants you to go to Rwanda and preach the gospel. How would you react? Would it be, "Oh, no! There has to be some mistake; and what about . . ."? That's right, there will be times when God will ask you to do the impossible, when He will ask you to commit an act which would seem to be like signing your own death warrant, when He will place you in an apparently unprotected state, with little or no visible means of provision or protection. That's how He sent out the apostles as shown in **Matthew 10**. Don't panic; instead, consider the following example from my life in business.

Personal Notes

Do not ask God to bless what you do. Instead find out what God wants you to do and do it. You will walk in His blessing without even asking for it.

Eternity waits for us, brothers and sisters. Let us do the bidding of our Saviour with eagerness and boldness. The night is far spent and all the host of heaven are preparing for the return of the King.

The reign of Satan is drawing to a close and all the peoples of the earth will one day share in our joy. In the meantime, let us announce the good news of the kingdom of God to every creature on this planet and bring the blessing of healing with every witness.

Do your part. Stand with your worldwide family and be a conduit of blessing to everyone you meet from now to the end of your days.

There are occasions when I need to send out one of my men to carry out a job for me. Now I consider myself to be a reasonable employer and I would take all the following into consideration when I do this. First, I would never ask someone to do something for me unless I had already done a similar job myself. Second, I would not send someone to do a job unless I was already confident of their ability to do it. Third, I would not expect this person to do the job on my behalf without my providing all the equipment and resources that person would need to carry out the job. Fourth, their safety and welfare are my responsibility and I would provide additional manpower if required and special equipment, if needed, to ensure their well-being.

Now that is for a work assignment in this world and from an imperfect human employer. Contrast that with a divine commission from God. Do you really believe, even for a moment, that God would not amply provide every conceivable provision?; that He would not go above and beyond what you even ask for or think?; that He would not send His angels with you and great empowerment through His Holy Spirit? **Jer 1** *"7But the Lord said to me: 'Do not say, I am a youth,' For you shall go to all to whom I send you, And whatever I command you, you shall speak. 8Do not be afraid of their faces, For I am with you to deliver you,' says the Lord. '19They will fight against you, But they shall not prevail against you. For I am with you,' says the Lord, 'to deliver you'."* Can you entertain the possibility that He would not grant you favour in the eyes of men and co-operation from the governing authorities? And as for anyone attempting to harm you, think of Daniel and the fiery furnace or in the lions' den. And what do you think would happen to you if you attempted to harm one of the children of the USA President? That would be an act of virtual suicide. So what do you suppose would happen to someone who tried to harm you? **Lk 17** *"2It would be better for him if a millstone were hung around his neck, and he were thrown into the sea, than that he should offend one of these little ones."*

So, back to you in Rwanda, probably with a team of other believers. You begin your commission in one of the smaller villages. You preach the gospel in English and the villagers hear you in their own language. Impossible? Well, who was it that confused the languages

Personal Notes

Do not ask God to bless what you do. Instead find out what God wants you to do and do it. You will walk in His blessing without even asking for it.

Eternity waits for us, brothers and sisters. Let us do the bidding of our Saviour with eagerness and boldness. The night is far spent and all the host of heaven are preparing for the return of the King.

The reign of Satan is drawing to a close and all the peoples of the earth will one day share in our joy. In the meantime, let us announce the good news of the kingdom of God to every creature on this planet and bring the blessing of healing with every witness.

Do your part. Stand with your worldwide family and be a conduit of blessing to everyone you meet from now to the end of your days.

in the first place? (**Genesis 11:9**) Who was it that brought under-standing to the visiting foreigners when they first heard the Apostles speak? (**Acts 2:6**).

You then explain about forgiveness of sins and that Christ will heal all those who come to Him and believe His report. So one or two approach; diseased, disabled, dying. You lay hands on them and instantly they're healed. As in Christ's day, the news will spread like wildfire.

You might say at this point. "Well, it doesn't really work that way any more. We preach the gospel, yes, but then we give out medicines and provide medical intervention for most, if not all, dis-tressing conditions. We build temporary shelters, provide food for the hungry, we dig water wells. We provide clothing, toys for the children, tools for the men so they can get back to work. We help rebuild infrastructure and provide comfort and counselling for the bereaved and the psychologically distraught. We set up truth and reconciliation commissions to hear grievances and provide a forum for accountability."

This goes back to what we were talking about earlier. No one denies that there are many options for people to choose when it comes to get-ting help. Christians from the west always have a medical option to pursue if they get sick and they receive according to their level of faith.

Today's world is infinitely more complex than at the time of Jesus' ministry, but the followers were actively engaged in providing for many of the practical needs of the poor and impoverished. They did not discriminate on the basis of the recipient's faith or belief. If that person needed help, even if they were an enemy of the church, the members were obligated to provide that help. Jesus actually com-manded that.

In some respects, the issues of human rights, socialist values and other human conventions have effectively hijacked Christian princi-

Personal Notes

Do not ask God to bless what you do. Instead find out what God wants you to do and do it. You will walk in His blessing without even asking for it.

Eternity waits for us, brothers and sisters. Let us do the bidding of our Saviour with eagerness and boldness. The night is far spent and all the host of heaven are preparing for the return of the King.

The reign of Satan is drawing to a close and all the peoples of the earth will one day share in our joy. In the meantime, let us announce the good news of the kingdom of God to every creature on this planet and bring the blessing of healing with every witness.

Do your part. Stand with your worldwide family and be a conduit of blessing to everyone you meet from now to the end of your days.

ples and applied them in a secular setting. This has led to a diminution of the role of the church in contemporary society.

The church in many countries is now institutionalised. The divine linkage in many ways has been lost. We have "professionals" in almost every sphere of church life. A modern-day minister must now have printed credentials, paperwork that can chart his career from a theological college to when he wrote his doctoral thesis on the Holy Spirit. The formula for selecting a candidate for a particular role, promotion or assignment is no longer based on determining the individual's character or assessment of his spiritual maturity, but on documented legitimacy.

What about divine appointment? In the present age, how does God endorse His followers so that the world will know who we are? All the answers are there in scripture and none of them come with any paperwork. "By their fruits you will know them!"

Need healing? Go see a doctor. Demon possessed? Go see a psychiatrist. Bereaved? Call a grief counsellor. Need salvation? Try a five-minute prayer and go to church on Sunday.

None of the above requires faith, or real life-changing commitments. These are the philosophies of the McChristian. Real Christianity has never been a religion. There is no fence straddling, no opting in and out. Either you're in or you're not. God loves faith. He responds to faith and He radically blesses the faithful. We can and should work within the existing world structures and actively approve, support and defend its best elements. But to be a balanced Christian you must pray for, expect to see and be a part of divine intervention in your own life and in the lives of others. For us, there is no such thing as a hopeless situation.

Live each day on that basis and you will come to understand why the Christian life is so much more than a job or a career choice. It really is a living, breathing, God ordained adventure! May the Lord Jesus Christ direct you in all your future steps.

Be a Witness for the Kingdom

If you have been brought to deliverance we would like to hear from you. Physical and mental affliction of any kind, whether it has happened to you directly or to someone close to you, is made worse by the feeling of isolation, that no one really knows what you are going through. Think how much your situation could have been eased by being able to confer with someone who has gone through exactly the same thing.

Here is your opportunity to serve the worldwide family that God has given you. Using the notes you compiled as you made your way through this book, write a report (not more than 250 words) about the process God took you through. Say what He revealed to you and how deliverance finally came. Be sure to include the information requested below, which is a necessary requirement for all testimonies presented to us. Interested secular authorities and the media must be able to validate your claims in order for your witness to be effective.

Once your witness statement has been authenticated, it will be showcased on our website as a genuine testimony of God's deliverance. Visitors to our website, who are suffering a similar affliction to your own and desire your prayers and personal support, will then be able to contact you using the information you provided.

How God leads you to assist them, from that point on, is up to you. Just remember, this level of service requires humility, faith, perseverance and sacrificial love. But the fruits of your labour will be truly eternal. May the riches of His grace inspire your actions.

TESTIMONY DETAILS:

Full Name

Location (e.g. town, region and country)

Contact details: (pick one): Telephone Number, E-mail address, Other (please describe).

Precise medical description of your affliction:

Date of diagnosis:

Place of diagnosis and/or treatment:

The name and profession of the physician who both diagnosed your condition and then witnessed the results of your healing:

Name of your church and the minister who counselled you:

Describe what God brought to your attention:

Date of deliverance and describe how it was manifested:

Conclude with a short message to those who will read your testimony.

E-mail your testimony through our website at: <www.godintercedes.com>

Thank you.

Personal Notes

Your witness means so much to the people out there. Please use this space to compile your report.

How to Be a Sponsor

It is a fact of life that individuals or families, afflicted by physical or mental distress, can often be financially challenged even within the Christian community. Rather than deprive them of a valuable resource that can promote their healing and bring about the deliverance they so desperately need, it was decided that this book should be made available to all regardless of their ability to pay.

Consequently, a sponsorship scheme was founded to enable this ambition to be realised. If you feel that your life has been radically blessed as a result of the messages contained within this book and you feel led by God to support this work, then your contributions would be greatly appreciated.

To become a sponsor, either log-on to our website at: <www.godintercedes.com> and use your credit or debit card, or telephone our office on: 0870-609-2336, or mail your cheque to: Premier Publications, P.O. Box 26623, Helensburgh, G84 4AH.

Please remember to include your name and address for our records and for us to forward a receipt to you.

Please note: We are not a registered charity and therefore contributions are not tax deductible.

Please indicate the total number of books you wish to sponsor on behalf of others. Now multiply the number of books by the purchase price of £12 (including post and packaging)

For accounting purposes, every sponsored copy will have a specific transaction number assigned to it. You will receive a receipt detailing the numbers assigned to each copy you sponsored.

In addition, we ask you to pray for those recipients of your generosity. That they may be blessed in their healing as you have been. Thank you for choosing to be a part of this ministry. May God prosper you in every area of your life.